Practicing the Here and Now

Being Intentional with Step 11

Using Prayer and Meditation to Work All the Steps

Herb K.

T0057454

Hazelden Publishing

Hazelden Publishing
Center City, Minnesota 55012
hazelden.org/bookstore

ISBN: 978-1-61649-674-6; ebook 978-1-61649-761-3

Library of Congress Cataloging-in-Publication Data is on file
with the Library of Congress.

Editor's notes:
This work respects the Twelfth Tradition of Alcoholics Anonymous, which
emphasizes anonymity as a foundation of the Twelve Step program. Names,
details, and circumstances may have been changed to protect the privacy of
those mentioned in this publication.

    This publication is not intended as a substitute for the advice of health
care professionals.

    Alcoholics Anonymous, AA, and the Big Book are registered trademarks
of Alcoholics Anonymous World Services, Inc.

25 24 23 22   4 5 6

Developmental editor: Sid Farrar
Production editor: Mindy Keskinen
Cover design by Linda Koutsky
Interior design and typesetting by Terri Kinne

To Mary Flanagan Kaighan, my wife;
mother of our three adult children;
grandmother to their seven.

You had the courage to open the door to your recovery and hold it open for me to follow. Little did we know it was the door to the world of Spirit—a world that had eluded each of us for more than forty years. Now we live there, our lives flourishing. Together we stand by the door, holding it open for others to enter into this world of freedom. We can't get here from there, but fifty years later, here we are. Thank you.

CONTENTS

Introduction

MEDITATION IS SIMPLE, but not easy! There is a lot of confusion and ignorance (not knowing) about what it is, how to do it, why to do it.

Multiple studies have shown that people who meditate regularly have less stress and generally have a better quality of life. But still, meditation has not been embraced consistently, even by a surprisingly large number of those people who are traveling on a general spiritual path or are members of an organized religion. Many people in the Twelve Step recovery community don't meditate either, even though their lives are alleged to be contingent on it. Nor do many seekers on the various paths of self-help, let alone anyone who is still lost in a morass of self-centered suffering.

The personal, physical, psychological, and spiritual values of meditation have not been understood or consistently applied by many people who could benefit most from a consistent meditation practice.

On the other hand, most people are familiar with and practice some form of prayer. But as common as prayer is in many people's daily lives, it is defined and practiced in so many ways that finding a shared understanding of what we mean by prayer can be a challenge, especially as it applies to the Twelve Steps.

• • •

Why This Book?

The purpose of this book is to provide an understanding of prayer and meditation as prescribed in Step Eleven of the Twelve Steps of Alcoholics Anonymous: "Sought through prayer and meditation to improve our conscious contact with God *as we understood Him,* praying only for knowledge of His will for us and the power to carry that out." This book offers readers in recovery clarity and practical guidance for a personal practice to improve their consciousness by learning to live in the here and now. It provides information that will help the reader understand both prayer and meditation, embrace the value of a daily practice, begin a consistent practice, and continue to experience an improvement in consciousness and behavior. It offers a lens for viewing each of the Twelve Steps from the perspective of Step Eleven prayer and meditation. Steps One and Two lay the foundation for the following Steps by showing us our inherent powerlessness and the source of our Power; the next ten Steps provide us with the means to connect with Power—and stay connected to it.

This book will address these key questions:

- What is meditation?
- What is prayer?
- Why do meditation? How and when do I do it?
- Why pray? How and when do I pray?
- What is the value, the specific benefit for me, of a consistent practice of prayer and meditation?
- What is the role of prayer and meditation in how we apply each of the Twelve Steps in our daily lives?

My hope is that this book will be a lantern shining the light of my experience on the path that I have walked, so that readers can navigate their own path with the benefit of this light.

Who Am I to Write This Book?

I've earned my credentials the hard way: through years of personal struggle, hard-won insight, and the gift of a spiritual awakening. In my early adulthood, I spent seven years of silence in a seminary; I did not really understand meditation, despite that contemplative setting. I then pursued a graduate education in psychology and, simultaneously, lots of personal therapy. Then I became a drunk for twenty years. I did not do meditation during this time, although I participated in many of the self-help opportunities of the 1960s, '70s, and '80s. Freed from alcohol in 1984, I came into a Twelve Step Fellowship and for four years I went to daily meetings; I still did not change. Finally, in my fifth year I worked and experienced *all* Twelve Steps; at last I changed and was changed, radically.

As a result of the application of the Twelve Steps, I was gifted with a spiritual awakening in 1988. I practiced the instructions on meditation in the Big Book of *Alcoholics Anonymous;* I became a daily meditator. I was certified as a spiritual director in 1989 and the next year Father Thomas Keating initiated me into a daily practice of contemplation via Centering Prayer. I have authored two books on Twelve Step spirituality: *Twelve-Step Guide to Using the Alcoholics Anonymous Big Book* (2004) and *Twelve Steps to Spiritual Awakening: Enlightenment for Everyone* (2010). The result of this Twelve Step process and my daily meditation practice has been a full and rewarding life for the last twenty-eight years—it flourishes.

My vision, purpose, and service philosophy is summed up in my mission: "To help others get on a spiritual path and stay on it."

The Power of Asking Questions

My primary approach is to stimulate questions that readers can ask themselves, so that their understanding will have personal significance.

I believe that questions are often more important than answers. It's my experience that when I'm given an answer before I have a real question—that is, before I know exactly what I'm hoping to learn—the answer has no place to reside and connect. But if I have truly asked myself a relevant question, then, in combination with some action on my part, the answer can produce an *experience.*

It was in the family program where my wife was being treated for her alcoholism that I was asked a question that turned my life around: "What is your autobiography of your relationship to alcohol?" I had never reflected on this aspect of my personal history. Despite seven years in seminary with monthly meetings with my spiritual director, weekly meetings with therapists for over twenty years, and a variety of self-help programs in between, I had never asked myself about, nor reviewed, my own history of drinking. When I reflected on this question, wrote out my memories, and read this reflection to a group of my peers, I began my journey of identifying the problem and awakening to the solution. I had an experience!

The hospital professionals knew I was an alcoholic. They also knew that I did not know and that I'd resist their pointing it out. So they asked me to ask myself the question of my historical experience. I was willing to accept this suggestion and to take the action.

Joe M. and Charlie P., who gained national notoriety in the 1980s and '90s for their weekend-long Big Book workshops, made it really simple. They advised us that you'd recognize a question by the question mark at the end of a sentence. Treat it as a stop sign. Stop. Pause. Hear the question. Ask the question of yourself. Reflect. Then, and only then, answer the question. I suggest you use this book the same way.

Father Richard Rohr, author and Franciscan priest, describes it this way: when we hold an unanswered question in the milieu of prayer and willingness, the question percolates. When we hold the question, get some information, take some action, we are brought to a new experience, which suggests an answer and perhaps a new question. This is the dynamic process of waking up. This is the formula for creating an experience.[1]

A spiritual awakening works like a dimmer switch on a light, a switch that moves one notch at a time. Since we're talking about the fourth dimension, the world of Spirit, this dimmer switch can move infinitely—there's no end to the spectrum. It does, however, move in both directions—forward and backward. It is my experience that the dimmer switch is spring-loaded to go backward. I need to lean into it to keep it moving forward. If I rest on my laurels, my past accomplishments, the dimmer switch will slowly move backward toward the dark side, one click at a time. The movement in either direction can be so gradual that it is not even noticed. But eventually, we realize we have more light and can see more, or we have returned to the darkness and suffer more.

Ask yourself: Am I walking in the Light or floundering in darkness? Is my life flourishing, or is my life one of serial suffering?

Approach this book in the spirit of questioning. Before reading each chapter, ask yourself, *Am I willing to open my mind and my heart?* Then, after reading the chapter, ask yourself these questions:

- What did it say?
- What does it mean?
- Do I have any experience with it?
- How does it apply to my personal life?
- What is the invitation?

The Spirit of "Setting Aside"

The Big Book of *Alcoholics Anonymous* suggests that we let go of our old ideas "absolutely" (page 58). As I started to work the Steps in my recovery, the man who guided me suggested that I set aside my prior information, experiences, and expectations. He quoted Albert Einstein: "The consciousness that created the problem cannot be the consciousness that solves the problem." That was probably Bill Wilson's insight as well, since the ultimate purpose of the Step process is a spiritual awakening as expressed in Step Twelve: "Having had a spiritual awakening as *the* result of these Steps . . . " (italics added).

This open-mindedness represents a major shift in consciousness. To the extent that I hold on to my prior knowledge, experiences, and perceptions of reality, I am blocked from having any different knowledge, correct perceptions, and new experiences. And I realize I am powerless to let go "absolutely." So I pray what I have come to call a *Set Aside prayer*:

> *Please set it all aside so that I can be taken to a place*
> *I have never been, a place I don't yet know exists.*

Another version:

> *Please release me from up to now,*
> *detach me from after now,*
> *and allow me to be fully present in the now.*

The Russian metaphysical philosopher G. I. Gurdjieff speculated that all humans are "asleep dreaming that we are awake." He believed that our primary task is to wake up. Can we wake up on our own power? To what extent have we managed to wake up, with all our past efforts? How successful have we been in discerning a better path? Even *knowing* better, how effective and consistent have we been in *doing* better?[2]

Similarly, the founder of psychoanalysis, Sigmund Freud, suggested that a person's primary task is to make the unconscious conscious. Otherwise, we might conclude that our life is a series of accidents driven by fate—that we are perennial victims. Or, we conclude, our life is subject to other people's selfishness and ill will, and we again are perpetual victims.

Whether you agree with these judgments or not, I invite you to at least take an attitude of neutrality and curiosity, bringing that approach to this book.

Ask yourself:

- How successful have I been to assure that I am accurately informed about life's meaning and purpose?
- How effective have I been in applying information or other people's experience to my personal life?
- Am I willing to receive new information, to be taken to a place that I might not even suspect is there?
- Am I willing to try on different attitudes, to take different actions, to have a new experience?
- Am I willing to change? Am I willing to *be* changed?

Suggestion: Create your own Set Aside prayer. It's not about the words; it's about the intent, the spirit, the attitude of openness. Each morning and anytime you begin to read this book, pray in your own words that any prior knowledge, any perceptions, any experiences that may block you from having new experiences, be set aside.

Entering the World of Spirit: Understanding Intentional Consciousness

Let's take a moment to see the broader context. Let's stand on the top of the mountain and get a panoramic view of the spiritual life, the path of improving our consciousness and enlarging our compassion. Steps One through Nine confirm our human brokenness. We live in a world of "selfishness—self-centeredness! That, we think, is the root of our troubles," says the Big Book (page 62).

Introducing Step Ten, the book declares we have now entered the world of Spirit and we commence a specific "way of living" (page 84). We continue to foster a relationship with Spirit "deep down inside." This daily practice of a new way of life helps ensure immunity from our addiction and freedom from the "bondage of self" as represented by the bedevilments (page 52). We have a daily reprieve: we have *recovered*; but we are not *cured*. We diligently practice our way of life and become channels of Spirit through Steps Ten, Eleven, and Twelve.

Way of Life: We keep the channel clear through our consistent practice of Step Ten: "continued to take personal inventory and when we were wrong promptly admitted it." The Twelve and Twelve confirms that inventory and meditation go hand in glove. Through inventory, we remove or minimize the shadows that block the "Sunlight of the Spirit." When *disturbed,* we take care of it on the spot. We identify and remove the disturbance by use of prayer, meditation, examination of consciousness, and action.

Intentional Consciousness: We fill the channel by practicing Step Eleven. The Big Book's first instruction on meditation is to do a nightly inventory. Thus, we pick up on our spiritual radar screen whatever *disturbance* was missed during the day and have it removed. We review and think about the day just lived, examining it for failures and successes. We prepare for tomorrow, committing to change and to repair any damage done today. The Big Book's second instruction is to have a morning practice of receiving specific *guidance* for the day and improving our relationship with Power. Thus, just for today, we are empowered to stay aligned with Spirit. "Thy will be done" is a prayer initiated by my free will. I pray to be enabled to *know* better and empowered to *do* better, a process of continued improvement of Intentional Consciousness.

What is Intentional Consciousness? It's my own term for fully understanding ourselves as humans. It's an umbrella phrase meant to be all inclusive of the historical human efforts to be awake, to develop awareness, and to improve conscience, consciousness, and conscious contact with, at the very least, the true human self and, at the very most, with the Mystery. It embraces practices such as prayer, meditation, contemplation, mindfulness, centering prayer, and many others.

Principles and Service: We share the contents of the channel by practicing Step Twelve: "Having had a spiritual awakening as the result of these steps, we tried to carry this message to alcoholics, and to practice these principles in all our affairs." We allow the contents of the channel to seep out into the community. This process develops over time, naturally. Spiritual principles manifest and guide us into a life of helping those around us, especially those in our Fellowship. This is an organic process of enlarging our spiritual life through the compassion we develop with Intentional Consciousness.

Meditation: Many paths, many goals

The history of human effort to understand human nature, to explain human purpose and meaning, to develop methods and processes for human improvement, has resulted in a variety of philosophies, psychologies, and theologies. And many of these worldviews developed some kind of meditation practice, by whatever name it might be called. Each approach carries a cultural tradition with it. And, for each practitioner, each approach carries meanings derived from one's own life: one's family of origin, cultural and educational influences, personal choices and experiences.

A popular writer on spiritual practice, Ken Wilber, speculates that everybody and everything is right: their explanations and conclusions are correct at their level of consciousness and evolutionary development. As humans walk higher up the mountain of our evolutionary development of consciousness, we are able to have a bigger view, a clearer and more comprehensive perspective of reality.[3]

Each approach to meditation is based on the purpose of the effort and underlying beliefs and assumptions about human nature and reality. I see four general approaches to the practice of meditation:

- Is it for physical health and stress reduction? Its value is *physiological.*
- Is it for emotional harmony, balance, and sense of well-being? Its value is *psychological.*
- Is it to establish and maintain satisfactory human relationships? Its value is *social and relational.*
- Is it to find and improve conscious contact with the Mystery? Its value is *spiritual, religious, or theological.*

We'll discuss meditation and prayer further in chapter 1.

What Makes Us Truly Human?

The two functions that make us truly human are our *mind* for thinking and our *free will* for making decisions and taking action. Over thousands of years of development, the human brain has evolved in three phases for survival:

- first, the *brain stem,* to coordinate our physical instincts
- second, the *limbic system* to govern our emotional responses
- third, the *cortex and neocortex* to regulate the functioning of our mind and will

I use the word *mind* here as a symbol of all the ways of knowing: thinking, intuition, inspiration, instinct, and sensing, not as a precise scientific term. *Mind* represents all human sources of awareness from the brain, heart, gut, five senses, and so on. It represents all the various ways of receiving information and discerning their meaning.

Among living beings, we humans are unique in the level to which we are aware that we are aware, that is, self-conscious. We can reflect on our history, project into the future, and currently think about the present moment. The function of the human mind is awareness and knowing, a function of language. The mind is always operating and is necessary for survival.

The word *will* is used here as the symbol of the function that allows humans to make a free choice, to make a voluntary decision, to select an alternative, and to take action—which are based on information received from the *mind*. This information is processed and becomes knowledge, our perception and interpretation of reality. Thus, we develop awareness of alternatives and assign values to these alternatives. Based on our perception of our own wants and needs, we make a choice and then take the action we've determined is appropriate. We'll discuss this further in chapter 2.

Mystery . . . as We *Don't* Understand It?

Earlier in this discussion I used the term *Mystery.* Why Mystery? Because we don't really know its nature. Is there a God, Higher Power, or Holy Spirit? Or is this mystery really only the human spirit, the collective unconscious introduced by psychologist Carl Jung; or perhaps the higher self of some Eastern religions; or the true self of current psychology?

And *if* there is this Larger Reality, what is *It,* and where?

Prayer is our heart-felt and mind-filled conversation with fourth dimension Spirit, Absolute Reality, the Ultimate Mystery.

Meditation is our diligent attention to our awareness of our thoughts and feelings as the direct communication of this Spirit to us.

Contemplation is our wordless, gentle, focused intention in the Presence of this Spirit: to acknowledge this Energy so as to be brought into ever-increasing conscious contact with Its Absolute Presence; to consent to this Energy so as to be shaped by this Reality; to realize our existential unity as an instrument and channel of healing.

I use the global term *Mystery* because we really don't know. In the Big Book chapter "We Agnostics," we read that if we have an authentic experience of powerlessness—having no choice—we then need some Power other than our personal power or even *any* human power. So we make a decision, an act of faith, that *It* exists!

Common sense confirms that we have no human words that adequately name *It*. *It* exists only as a Reality in the fourth dimension, the world of Spirit. This Reality cannot be captured in words coming from a three-dimensional, material reality. Fortunately, the Big Book suggests we choose our own words for *It* and for our relationship with whatever we call it—the silver bullet of Steps Two and Three. (More about that in chapter 3.)

How to Get the Most Out of This Book

The object of this book is to fit you with a new pair of glasses—prayer and meditation (in the words of Chuck C.'s classic book

A New Pair of Glasses). These lenses will give you new insight into each Step. I also hope that they'll help you focus on a path that will result in a *new* experience with each Step. Lean gently into it, invite the Spirit to embrace you and draw you forward. This is not an event, but a process; this is not a task to be finished, but a path to be walked.

This book will provide you with information—more knowledge. It is possible it could also precipitate transformation—an experience that changes you. To maximize the impact of this book:

- *Come to it with the Set Aside spirit.* At the very least, this is a positive affirmation of holding an open mind and heart. At the very most, it is an outreach to a Power other than our own for help. Each chapter begins with a cue for a Set Aside prayer.

- *Read with intention and curiosity.* This is not a book to be just read and finished—a task. This is a discussion to be engaged in and experienced—a process.

- *Pause when asked questions.* You'll find a set of reflective questions at the beginning of each chapter and elsewhere too. Take the time to reflect and then write a response, either on paper or on screen. Be radically honest with yourself; be willing to be surprised.

- *Keep a copy of the Big Book handy.* You'll see many references to it; the in-text page numbers refer to the fourth edition, published in 2001. Reading the recommended passages will greatly enhance the value of this book.

- *Use other resources.* If possible, keep *Twelve Steps and Twelve Traditions* (the "Twelve and Twelve") at hand too. Use a dictionary to ponder the meanings of key words. If parts of this book are difficult to understand on first reading,

To live in God as fish in water, not always awake but totally
dependent for survival.

To aspire to a shift in consciousness, even a tiny one.

To know what I think, when I'm thinking.

To know what I'm feeling, to feel what I'm feeling.

To not resist what I'm feeling, but to acknowledge and
even embrace these feelings.

To take actions through deliberate choice.

To be present to the moment and to those who witness
that moment.

To sense my dependence in each of these moments and
trust that I'm deeply loved and totally taken care of.

To surrender and fall backward into the abyss of the
underlying Soul of the Universe.

And to know that it's gift—all gift.

And to be grateful!

This is my practice.

To be patient and compassionate with my dullness, my
ignorance, my willfulness, my sloth, my
self-indulgence.

And to understand and accept that this is also my practice.

To live in God as fish live in water, neither clinging nor
resisting.

To come to consciousness, to be awake, to be aware, to be
present to the present moment.

To live in now—not yesterday; not tomorrow.

Moving with the flow. Breathing in. Breathing out.

Aware of and focused only on the sacred now.

This is my practice.

come back to them—this is a journey, not a destination. If possible, discuss what you're reading with others who are traveling a spiritual path.

If you sincerely embrace all these approaches, you will have a new experience and be taken to a place you do not even suspect is available.

A spiritual awakening is the promise of Step Twelve. It is a radical change in the way we think, feel, and behave. It is done *to* us, not *by* us. At the same time, we contribute to it by being willing, open-minded, and honest while taking the necessary action. We are willing to be taken to a place of willingness; we are willing to be taken.

We co-create this experience of awareness through our willingness and the gift of Grace. At the beginning, we contribute substantially through our cooperation and action; at the end, we realize that the outcome and results are disproportionately larger than our contribution to them. At the beginning, we incorporate meditation and prayer into our journey to support the Step process of awakening; at the end, meditation and prayer have become an integral practice for improving and enlarging this awakening.

The journey is the destination!

. . .

Note: Each chapter of this book ends with an exercise or other call to action. To get the most out of this book, apply yourself to each of these before reading further.

Prepare to Practice Intentional Consciousness

Your first assignment prepares you for **Intentional Consciousness** through prayer and meditation.

1. Choose the Set Aside prayer that works best for you right now. Let's repeat the two versions mentioned earlier; you'll find others in appendix A of this book.

   - *Please set it all aside so that I can be taken to a place I have never been, a place I don't yet know exists.*

   - *Please release me from up to now, detach me from after now, and allow me to be fully present in the now.*

   From now on, pray your Set Aside prayer every morning, to begin a modest prayer practice. Whenever you read this book, pray it as you begin each exercise, that you might complete it with an open mind, open heart, and attitude of humility.

2. Before reading chapter 1, consider Step Twelve:

   Having had a spiritual awakening as the result of these steps, we tried to carry this message to alcoholics, and to practice these principles in all our affairs.

   Focus on the purpose and promise of the Twelve Step process: *to have a spiritual awakening.*

continued

In the Big Book, read pages 567–68 and consider the meaning of both a spiritual awakening and a spiritual experience. Ask yourself:

What do these terms mean? How are they the same? How do they differ?

3. In the Big Book, carefully read the instructions on prayer and meditation, pages 85–88.

Being clear on the mission and incorporating these tools of Intentional Consciousness improves the power and effectiveness of the process.

· · ·

1

Prayer and Meditation as Intentional Consciousness

STEP ELEVEN

Step Eleven	*Sought through prayer and meditation to improve our conscious contact with God* as we understood Him, *praying only for knowledge of His will for us and the power to carry that out.*

To prepare for this chapter

Review the Set Aside prayer discussed in the introduction. Reflect on how you might adapt the prayer for your own use as you read this book. Each chapter will begin with a cue to use the Set Aside prayer.

Keep these questions in mind

Please ask, hold, and reflect on these questions; only then write your answers in your journal for this book.

- Is prayer important to you? Is meditation important to you?
- Why? What is their importance to you?
- Do you pray? Do you meditate? How often?
  What exactly do you do?
- If you don't have a consistent, daily practice, why not?
- Do you want to have a consistent, daily practice?
  Why? What would be the value to you?
- Do you really believe all of what you just wrote?

We "have tapped an unsuspected inner resource . . ."
— BIG BOOK, page 567

IF YOU CAN THINK, you can meditate.

If you can speak (at least internally), you can pray.

Meditation and prayer are not complicated, mysterious, esoteric, or even very difficult. They come from the natural function of the human mind to think and the human heart to want, to desire. We cannot stop the mind from thinking, or the heart from desiring. These are their normal functions. However, we can manage, influence, channel, and observe our stream of thoughts and wants.

What's the difference between meditation and prayer? It's a matter of our intent. Are we *paying attention* to our thoughts? Or are we *communicating* them?

When we have thoughts and/or feelings with the intent of *paying attention to them, we are meditating*. Three definitions help us trace the meaning of the word: The Latin word *meditatio* means "To practice or exercise thought; to consider" (*Cassell's Latin Dictionary*). Later, the English word was defined as "to ponder, cogitate, reflect, to fix one's attention upon a specific thought, problem, or issue" (*Winston's Dictionary*, 1930). A more recent one is "deep thought, serious, continuous contemplation, esp. on a religious or spiritual theme" (*Wordsworth's Concise English Dictionary*, 2007).

What, then, is prayer? When we have thoughts and/or feelings with the intent of *communicating* them, we are praying. Revisiting the same sources, the Latin *precor; precatio; preces* means "to speak to another; to beg, request, wish; to promise, vow; to sing a supplication, a gratitude, or a thanksgiving." Later sources give us "to speak to God; earnest entreaty; implore; beg; request thanks and praise; a form of worship; earnest appeal on behalf of another" and "to make known one's desires to God; to ask reverently; to express sincere devotion."

Some Historical Background

When Bill Wilson and Bob Smith founded Alcoholics Anonymous in 1935, they both had an experience of prayer and meditation shaped by the Oxford Group. Originally known as A First Century Christian Fellowship, the Oxford Group was started in 1921 by Lutheran minister Frank Buchman and was later led by Episcopalian minister Sam Shoemaker. Its purpose was to bring authentic spirituality back into the Christian churches. The Oxford Group developed a process for personal transformation whose six steps were later adapted by the early AA fellowship and referred to in one of the stories in the Big Book (page 263):

1. Complete deflation
2. Dependence and guidance from a Higher Power
3. Moral inventory
4. Confession
5. Restitution
6. Continued work with others

Bill W. came to the Oxford Group through a chain of referrals. In 1933, a man named Roland Hazard found the group as he was following the suggestion of Dr. Carl Jung "to find a spiritual experience" to overcome his alcoholism (Big Book, pages 26 and 27). Using the Oxford Group steps, Roland found freedom from alcohol. Following the final suggestion, he reached out to another alcoholic, Ebby Thatcher. Ebby worked these six steps and he, too, was released from his addiction. Then Ebby contacted his former drinking buddy, Bill Wilson, who he had heard was deeply troubled by booze. Bill worked these six steps while hospitalized and soon thereafter had a spiritual experience (Big Book, pages 13–14).

Bill carried this message to Dr. Bob Smith, who had already been in the Oxford Group for two and a half years. Bob had gone to weekly meetings in which he read the Bible, prayed, and joined the discussions. After each of these weekly meetings, he went home and got drunk.

Bob was sitting in the solution, but did not know the nature of the problem. He thought alcoholism was a moral issue, a knowledge issue, a willpower issue. When Bill explained what he'd learned from Dr. William Silkworth—that alcoholism is an allergy of the body and an obsession of the mind—and he described his own experience of powerlessness and receiving Power, Dr. Bob " . . . began to pursue the spiritual remedy for his malady with a willingness he had never before been able to muster" (Big Book, page xvi).

This is the background that led to the founding of AA and the writing of the Big Book (1939) and *Twelve Steps and Twelve Traditions* (1953). It reveals a specific understanding about prayer and meditation and a specific structure and process for doing it.

Meditation is "directed thinking." It is a methodology using the human faculty of thinking and knowing to discern *guidance*—both for the day and also for one's life. We practice listening to the "wee small voice" deep inside our self. For people in Twelve Step recovery especially, it includes inventory in the evening, planning in the morning, and awareness throughout our waking day.

The Big Book gives very clear instructions about prayer and meditation on pages 85–88. This approach by the first hundred AA members came out of their Oxford Group experience. Look at the specific instructions for morning meditation on page 86:

On awakening, let us think about the twenty-four hours ahead. We consider our plans for the day. Before we begin, we ask God to direct our thinking...

This way of speaking in the Big Book is a code. It suggests talking to God/Higher Power. We are *asking* for direction. Obviously, the assumption is that we actually *have* a positive concept of God or a Higher Power. A concept that includes being present, listening, caring, power, responsiveness, and effectiveness. (More on this in chapter 3.) Here we see prayer and meditation closely linked in a process of asking for help and listening for what form that help will take.

With our free will, we choose to acknowledge this Reality and ask for help (in prayer). To ask for help is intentional—with purpose, focus, choice, and with our free will we are asking for and consenting to receive help. We listen for that help, paying attention and elevating our consciousness (in meditation).

What Is Prayer?

As the AA founders taught us, prayer is a request for assistance, for help to know: *What is the solution to a problem?* and *What is the best alternative as a course of action?*

Prayer is a recognition of our need for some power more than our own, our need to be empowered to make a choice and to take the action indicated by that choice. Whatever it is, it is our effort, based on our own free will, to take the action of becoming more conscious. Prayer most effectively uses words not to express our wants and needs, but to ask for the best course of action, to become more conscious.

Prayer may be a request to a Power other than our self, if that matches our belief system. Prayer could also be seen as a positive affirmation of the potential of our human consciousness to address our higher self. Dr. Allen Berger describes this as "the worst in us is reaching out to the best in us." We are calling on our true self, the innate core of natural goodness that is the life force underneath our fabricated self.

Prayer is an intimate conversation with consciousness (ours, humanity's, or the Mystery's—you choose). Effective prayer is thought-*full*, not rote recitation. Effective prayer is soul-*full*, not empty ritual.

Something happens as the result of our effort. We're really not sure why it happens. We are sure *that* it happens—it does definitely have an impact on our lives.

At the very least, it is the power of positive thinking and affirmation. This ancient wisdom has been expressed in many ways, from William James's "healthy mindedness" in *The Varieties of Religious Experience*, a book that strongly influenced Bill W.; to Emmett Fox's books, including *The Sermon on the Mount*, still read by many in the AA fellowship; and more recently in the best-seller *The Secret* by Rhonda Byrne and its spinoff movie. The hundreds of self-help books espousing a positive psychology have demonstrated the effectiveness of positive attitude, a habit of gratitude, and association with people with these dispositions.

At the very most, it may be a mystical connection to the source of all reality so that we're aligned with the flow of positive energy and life force.

Bottom line: prayer is our conscious request for help, expressed either out loud or in silence. We don't need to know how it works. We don't need to believe that it actually *will* work. We just need to do it! And then, down the road, we may look back over our shoulder and appreciate that it *did* work (whatever that may mean to you).

Prayer does not change God or reality; it changes the pray-*er*.

What Is Meditation?

If prayer is a form of speaking, meditation can be seen as a form of intense listening. I define meditation here as the process of thinking about a prayer request and paying attention to our thinking/feeling. We'll consider other definitions of meditation later in this book.

We don't listen for words spoken to our ears. We listen for awarenesses whispered to our *mind*: our thoughts, inspirations, intuitions, instincts. We listen with all our heart and awareness for the "wee small voice" of guidance: a sense, a feeling, a knowing, a hearing.

- We ask (pray) that our Higher Power direct our thinking. Then we begin thinking.
- We listen/pay attention (meditation) to our thoughts, trusting they are a direct response to our prayer.
- We trust we are receiving guidance about our activities today ("think about the twenty-four hours ahead").
- We trust we are receiving guidance for our attitude today ("consider our plans for the day").

We trust that all this is real—we trust the process and that we will receive communication that will help us answer the request or the question that was posed. We trust our self and that we will receive an indication of possible solutions to the problem or question that was presented—a process of discernment (thinking in the milieu of prayer).

We don't *know* if it is real; we have no certitude. We don't necessarily have any *feeling* that it is real. We may have no feelings, or we may even have feelings of resistance and doubt. But we have *faith*—a decision that it is so, and so we do it anyway. This doing is trust, behaving "as if it is true." Faith is a decision based not on knowledge or feeling, but on trust.

Meditation is an intentional process that allows us to receive *guidance*. That's why I have called this process Intentional Consciousness. *You* choose the belief system about the source of this guidance.

The value of meditation

As previously indicated, there are many valid reasons for practicing meditation as Intentional Consciousness:

- Physical health: It improves the immune system and overall biological function.

- Emotional health: It reduces stress and creates balance and harmony.

- Mental health: It reduces confusion and generates clarity/insight for appropriate action.

- Spiritual health: It reduces shadows by bringing light into our animating life force and fostering connection with our higher self/human spirit/Holy Spirit.

You choose your focus.
You choose what to accept.
You choose what to believe!

The Twelve and Twelve establishes the basic value proposition for a practice of consistent meditation. Physical health is compared with spiritual health. As air, water, food, and sunshine are vital for the body, prayer and meditation—Step Eleven—are the ingredients that nourish and sustain our spirit.

The Big Book is clear that we have a spiritual malady: "Selfishness—self-centeredness! That, we think, is the root of our troubles" (page 62). The Twelve Steps are a process of diagnosis and treatment for our spiritual disease. Steps Eleven and Twelve are specifically designed as the antidote: becoming other-centered.

Steps One through Nine are the tools for excision: soul surgery. If our basic problem is manifest as "bedevilments," the first nine Steps are a method of exorcism. Then Step Ten keeps our channel clean; Step Eleven fills our channel; Step Twelve allows our life-filled and overflowing channel to seep out to help the human community around us.

Step Eleven meditation becomes the daily *medication*.
Step Twelve provides *immunization*.

Most people, especially those awake to the need for a spiritual path, agree that meditation is very important. But very few people actually have a consistent practice. I believe their essential problem is that they have not established a real and personal value proposition for themselves. People won't do meditation just because they "should," or just because they're committed Twelve Steppers, or it is time to work Step Eleven, or their sponsor suggests it. *They will do it only when they establish a visceral value for doing it.*

Perhaps a new experience with Steps One, Two, and Three would be helpful. A truly new experience, not just a revisit! Ask yourself: Do I really concede to my innermost self that I am powerless on my own? Not just powerless over my addiction (first half of Step One), but over effectively managing my life on my own (second half of Step One). We'll be looking more deeply at these Steps in chapters 2 and 3.

Ask yourself these questions:

- Do I concede my powerlessness to my innermost self?
- What do I actually believe about a Power greater than myself and its availability to me?
- Do I need guidance and Power on a daily basis?
- Am I willing to go to any length to become and stay awake?

- Although I may have recovered, do I believe that I am not cured and that I have only a daily reprieve contingent on the maintenance of my spiritual condition?
- Do I have the personal power to know what to do to stay in alignment with my Higher Power's will?
- Do I have the personal power to actually do what I know is the right and healthy action to take?

Look at your feet for the truth: What do you actually do? What you *think* may be a delusion; what you actually *do* is the truth! Measure your belief against your behavior. Is there dissonance?

If you want a practice of meditation, establish a real value that is experience-based, and then begin practicing. As you will see later, you can start by committing to just *one minute a day* of Intentional Consciousness. This is not reading or praying. This is asking for our thoughts to be directed, and then thinking and listening to our thoughts as *the* direction.

One minute each day for thirty days. If you miss a day, start the count over. It may take ninety days to get there. But when you do, you will have begun a practice, will have developed the beginnings of a habit, will have started a journey that will change your life if continued.

Reading as meditation

The Twelve and Twelve offers a different method for beginning a meditation practice. It suggests we begin by thoughtfully reading a prayer or passage from an inspirational book compatible with Twelve Step principles. Read it one word or one phrase at a time and pause. Think about it. Consider it. Reflect deeply on this word or phrase:

- What did it say?

- What does it mean?
- Do I have any experience with it?
- How does it apply to my personal life?
- What is the invitation?

The purpose of this practice is not to simply finish the prayer or reading. The purpose is to focus our attention, to train our mind, to channel our thoughts into the fourth dimension. We must pay attention and listen to our thoughts. We must hear them as direct communication from our Higher Power, as a response to our prayer: "Please direct my thinking." We receive guidance if we want it and take the action of active listening.

Remember: We don't actually have to know how it works, or even believe that it will work. We just have to do it. Down the road, after a period of faithful practice, when we look back over our shoulder, we will see and know that it really does work.

What does it mean to have a practice?

Years ago, as I started my journey of transformation through the Twelve Steps, I made a commitment to seek Power through a meditation practice. But it was unsatisfying. I was frustrated with the perceived emptiness of my fifteen-minute sit each morning for a whole year.

I spoke with my spiritual director and, although not in a Twelve Step program, he understood mine, and he got Step One. He remarked that I was making my meditation a task to be accomplished, whereas it is a process to be experienced. He suggested I was trying to make something happen: to become spiritual, to become a good meditator.

"Herb, listen, please," he said. "The spiritual life is not like that; meditation doesn't respond like that. Think these thoughts: *I am as powerless over my spiritual life as I am over alcohol—having no power at all.* And, *I am as powerless over my meditation as I am over alcohol—having no power at all.* Sit in the Presence of Power humbled by your personal powerlessness. Your job is the effort. The results will be what they are."

Wow! That helped me drop the cement coat of responsibility for making spirituality happen. I am responsible for the effort. The results will take care of themselves. Freedom!

He continued: "There are only two mistakes you can make in meditation: *not show up!* and *leave early!* Everything in between is none of your business."

Before I left his office that day, he suggested, "If you want to know if your meditation practice is effective, after three months of consistent daily practice, ask your wife how you are treating her; pay attention to how you are driving on the highways; watch how you interact with retail personnel or food servers at restaurants. A consistent meditation practice will change you: you'll be more aware, more sensitive, kinder, more compassionate, less reactive, and more responsive."

How do I begin to meditate?

Most teachers recommend establishing a routine and an environment. After all, at our basic level we are animals subject to conditioning. I do my meditation around the same times each day, and in the same place. I have a ritual for beginning:

- Pray my Set Aside prayer, to have an open mind and heart.

- Repeat Step Eleven as my intent—a reminder of the mission, the purpose for this sitting "to improve my conscious contact . . ."

- Pray the Step Three prayer (Big Book, page 63), to align with life's flow:

    "God, I offer myself to Thee—to build with me and to do with me as Thou wilt. Relieve me of the bondage of

self, that I may better do Thy will. Take away my difficulties, that victory over them may bear witness to those I would help of Thy Power, Thy Love, and Thy Way of life. May I do Thy will always!"

- Use the meditation practice as outlined in the Big Book (pages 85–88)—asking for guidance and power to follow through; paying attention; directing the mind; listening to the "wee small voice."

- You might want to incorporate a contemplation practice, as I do—acknowledging Presence and consenting to let *It* have *Its* way with me; renewing intention; directing my will; being willing to be shaped by the Life Force. (This is drawn from the practice of Centering Prayer.)

- Finish with the Step Seven prayer (Big Book, page 76), which concludes,

  "Grant me strength, as I go out from here, to do your bidding."

  What a great launching pad for the day!

See appendix A for a fuller outline of my own Step Eleven prayer and meditation practice. This is my practice; each person has to design their own. I am very practical about making suggestions to others about starting a practice and to meet them where they are. I ask, "What are you willing to do? What will you commit to do? What will you actually do?"

Again, just start with one minute; build to five, then ten, then fifteen, then twenty minutes. Most teachers recommend a twenty- to thirty-minute sit each morning. Once this has been established and has become a habit, perhaps explore a second sit in the afternoon or evening. In the beginning, the use of a timer may be helpful to neutralize the distraction of concern for the clock.

The Big Book suggests two sits a day: *morning guidance*, a gathering of knowledge and power for the day; and *nightly review*, an inventory of the day.

During the day we attempt to stay awake, aware of the unconditional Love of God and the perpetual Presence of "a Spirit of the Universe underlying the totality of things" (Big Book, page 46). The Big Book recommends what might be the perfect prayer, "Thy will be done!" With my free will, I choose to align my free will and my behavior with my understanding of God's will for me at this present moment. All spiritual literature, no matter the tradition, embraces the benefits of living in the present moment. It is the only moment we actually have, and to the extent that we are present here and now, we create (or co-create) our destiny. Some Eastern religions teach the idea of karma, which I define as the effect of the accumulated impact of the decisions we make and actions we take, each moment of our consciousness (or unconsciousness!).

——————— The Practice of Consciousness ———————

Meditation is not just about stress reduction, feeling good, or especially making notes for quotable quotes. Meditation is not about becoming something or someone: not a good meditator, and certainly not an enlightened being. Meditation is about becoming awake to the contact with the Mystery, Power, Spirit, Guidance that already exists, and becoming fully conscious of our inherent oneness.

The delusion of difference dissolves ... through presence to Presence, in communion to union.

This is an organic metamorphosis of consciousness—caterpillar to butterfly. Our awareness of unity unfolds. Our action of compassion manifests. This is our practice of *Intentional Consciousness*.

The principal purpose of meditation is to maximize our consciousness. As we walk up the mountain of awareness, we have new vistas. But if we don't *see* that we have alternatives, we don't have them. If we see that we have alternatives, we can select one based on our evaluation of its benefit to ourselves. If we make a mistake in our selection and we see the mistake, we can correct it with a healthier alternative.

With more consciousness, we see more. The bad news: our walk on the path is erratic and flawed with many obstacles. The good news: our path has light to illuminate the obstacles so that we may trudge forward.

What are some of the keys to meditation?
Meditation is not a method. It is an attitude of being awake, hopeful, expectant; yet patient. Being grateful and compassionate. Being forgiving (or willing to be). Being present in the moment, present to the Presence.

In humility, we meditate, knowing ourselves to be all too human. In gratitude, we are thankful that we're able to meditate at all.

We meditate to invite the Spirit of the Universe to inform us, to conform us, and to inevitably transform us. This is a process of turning—from the bondage of self-centeredness to the freedom of other-centeredness.

Most spiritual traditions suggest that sincere seekers have three components to their journey. Consider these as you start or continue your own:

1. *A path.* Look for a method you resonate with, one that is simple, that makes common sense, and for which there is actual evidence that it works and achieves the purpose for your interest.

2. *A teacher.* Find someone who has experience that can shed light on the path, guide you, and who can help with accountability. It might be someone from your Twelve Step program or from your spiritual tradition, if you have one. Learn from that person's experience: successes and mistakes.

3. *A community.* All humans are social animals and do better when connected. As pilgrims on this lonely path of consciousness development, we find encouragement, support, and even opportunities for service in the context of a like-minded community. This can be your Twelve Step support groups, a spiritual community, or both, with daily, weekly, monthly, or periodic group functions.

What about posture and position?

Prayer and meditation are not about ritual. They are about *attention*: what are we thinking, wanting, needing? They are about *intention*: what is our attitude, our motive, our consciousness?

As for physical posture, some people sit in a chair or on a cushion. Some people stand or kneel. We don't stand or kneel to get God's attention; we stand or kneel to get *our* attention. Standing is a position of respect; kneeling is a posture of humility. My Step guide said he knelt to pray as an act of subordination, embodying his powerlessness and need of Power.

When sitting, most teachers recommend:

- body relaxed, back straight, feet on the floor
- hands comfortably in the lap, palms up or down
- eyes closed, open, or half open—be comfortable
- breathing in and out: slow, deep, deliberate, gentle, rhythmic, conscious

- mind open, aware, undefended, with *attention,* acknowledging Presence: our own faith decision, choice, concept
- heart (will, spirit) open, loving, and with *intention,* consenting to the invitation, the energy, and the action of the Reality in whose Presence we are sitting

In the words of Rabbi Heschel, "We don't meditate to become good meditators; we meditate to improve our conscious contact with G_d." (Heschel honored the Jewish tradition of referring to the deity only indirectly.)

What about distractions?

Our mind is a thinking machine. Our limbic system produces a constant barrage of feelings. Our memory lets loose a potpourri of images from the past. Our imagination is constantly visiting the future, creating short documentaries of potential opportunities and pitfalls. The obstacles to meditation (focused thinking) are innumerable.

We listen deeply to our thinking to hear and get guidance. Distractions come and go and come again. We stay attentive and intentional:

- neither resisting nor rejecting them
- neither clinging to nor detaching from them
- observing them flowing, like debris in a moving river
- noticing but not engaging with them
- remembering our intent for being here: to improve *conscious* contact
- when distracted, using our breath or sacred word to return to our center

This process and practice disciplines us; it gives us structure, guidance, energy, and even accountability. Be patient with yourself. Breathe in and out, deeply, slowly, rhythmically. Breathe in

Spirit; breathe out self. Breathe in Power; breathe out powerlessness. Breathe in the vision of guidance; breathe out the various dissipations. One breath at a time, refocus on paying attention and deeply listening.

My own teachers have suggested also using a sacred word as a symbol of my intent to be present. It acts as an anchor that brings me back to the Presence—Spirit, Power, and Guidance—in the present moment. The word is sacred because it is the word I've chosen for this practice. It has no inherent sacred value, meaning, or feeling. It is merely the symbol of my commitment to be awake and stay focused. It is a symbol of my belief about Presence—about Power, Spirit, and Guidance. It was a symbol of my consent to be shaped.

When distracted (any awareness other than the awareness of Presence), I invoke the sacred word and softly repeat it as a reminder of my commitment to watch and listen. *No* violence. *No* strained effort. *No* judgment. Trappist monk Father Thomas Keating, elaborating on the practice of Centering Prayer, describes the use of the sacred word as "placing a feather on a cotton ball." It is a very gentle effort to brush away all distractions and to return to Presence, watching, listening, and consenting.

Tapping in to the energy

Most people on a spiritual path have some kind of spiritual practice, however informal or rigorous. If they are faithful to their practice, then their practice is faithful to them.

Having a practice is like going to the gym. At first we need a lot of coaching, motivating, and perhaps some accountability system. It is hard work. After some consistency we are over the soreness and awkwardness and begin to enjoy the physical results. Soon we're in good shape and it feeds our sense of well-being and

---- To Discern (and to Become) the Message ----

In meditation, I sit in the Presence of Power, actively engaged,

With all my mind in thinking, listening, and discerning the message:

    focus = attention.

With all my will in loving, consenting, aligning, and becoming the message:

    focus = intention.

In meditation, I sit humbly in the presence of Power:

    to inform my mind:
    " . . . praying for the knowledge of God's will . . ."

    to empower my will:
    " . . . praying . . . for the power to carry it out."

---

self-esteem. We need less coaching, are self-motivated, and need very little structured accountability. We have acquired the desire and the skill. It's like learning a musical instrument, learning to dance, learning to ride a bicycle, or learning any other skill or discipline.

Meditation is our effort to align with the evolving and unfolding of life's energy. We need to be still and listen to this silent flow of energy. We need to dial in and place our awareness on the frequency of this energy flow.

I like the analogy of the battery-driven golf cart. All day long the job of the golf cart is to deliver golfers to the various tees. At night it is hooked up to a battery charger to restore power. Without that, the golf cart will be useless the next day, unable to fulfill its purpose. All night, it sits passively absorbing power. The next day, it is ready for service.

"We have tapped an unsuspected inner resource," says the Big Book (pages 567–68). Sometimes when I sit I have the mental image of a well. I drill down deep into the Life Force Energy Field. I am attempting to improve my conscious contact. I tap in and become acutely aware that I am already in constant contact: separation is a delusion. I am Source—saturated with the Life Energy.

There is no place that there is not God.

In the following chapters, let's take a deep look at each of the Twelve Steps through the lens of prayer and meditation. We'll review the Big Book instructions, and add some other ideas for applying each Step to our personal lives. We'll view prayer and meditation as tools for making the process more effective and the outcome more powerful.

When we look at an object with our naked eyes, we see only what our eyes will allow us to see. Our perception is actually shaped by our genetics, our family of origin, our adolescent and early adulthood education, our culture, and our overall life experiences. We don't see reality as it objectively is; we see reality as we subjectively are.

When we look through a magnifying lens, we see lots more depth and detail. When we look through a prism, we see a variety of colors not available to the unaided eyes.

When we look through the lenses of prayer and meditation, we are given the gift of being taken beyond our capacity to know and see; we are taken to a place we do not even know exists. With this new pair of glasses, we are given a brand-new experience of reality as *it* really is and may even encounter Reality as *It* really is.

. . .

— EXERCISE —

Personal Commitment to Action

Please ask yourself these questions and reflect for a time. Then write your answers in your paper or electronic journal:

- *What is my commitment to a prayer and meditation practice?*

- *How will I hold myself accountable to that commitment?*

• • •

2

We Become Conscious of Having "No Choice"

STEP ONE

Step One	*We admitted we were powerless over alcohol—that our lives had become unmanageable.*

To prepare for this chapter

Pray your version of the Set Aside prayer discussed in the introduction, putting aside all your prior information, experiences, and expectations with respect to Step One.

Keep these questions in mind

- What does it mean to be human? Who and/or what are we, essentially?
- What does it mean to know and decide?
- What is the nature of Step One and the meaning of "no power of choice"?
- Can we have a new experience of powerlessness in body, mind, and will?

"We learned that we had to fully concede to our innermost selves that we were alcoholics."

— BIG BOOK, page 30

IN THIS CHAPTER, we focus on Step One. Let's consider it in two parts.

First half: "*We admitted we were powerless over our addiction . . .*" (here we use the word *addiction* rather than *alcohol,* for broadest application). We feel that powerlessness in our *body* as craving (what the "Doctor's Opinion" chapter of the Big Book refers to as an allergy) and in our *mind* as obsession and delusion.

Second half: "*—that our lives had become unmanageable.*" We had tried to manage our lives through our own self-centered will, to no avail.

The Oxford Group called this self-centered will a "cancer of the soul." Twelve Step work is a process of "soul surgery," of excision. We are addressing the human deficiencies described as "bedevilments" in the Big Book (page 52); it can be seen as a process of exorcism. This is the human spiritual malady described by the Big Book as the root of inherent human brokenness (page 62). The Twelve Step methodology provides a path, a process of healing, of repairing our relationships with God or Higher Power, with self, with others. The source of the spiritual problem is a defective human will. My will, on my own power, seems to choose only me, my interests, my self, defending and fostering my ego. I am the conscious and unconscious center of my universe. This is a spiritual process of turning and being turned to realize humility—a perspective of truth. I am not the center of the universe.

Perhaps the evolution of our brain provides a model for understanding an approach to prayer and meditation, to the Step process, and to the spiritual life. It may also reveal a model for an understanding of Step One "Powerless"—no choice: physically, mentally, spiritually! Let's review what we discussed earlier:

- The *brain stem* is the basic "lizard brain," providing survival instincts for our physical system: body and instincts.

- The *limbic system* improves our survival odds by monitoring our relationships with self and others: feelings and intuitions.

- The *cortex/neocortex* provides further survival tools that give us language and consciousness. This final brain development distinguishes us as human beings with two unique functions: *mind,* the ability to self-reflect, conceptualize, imagine, create, think, gain insight, and transcend our self and the world around us; and *will,* the ability to make a voluntary decision and to act on it, free choice and deliberate action.

The Big Book supports this model: " . . . we have been not only mentally and physically ill, we have been spiritually sick. When the spiritual malady is overcome, we straighten out mentally and physically" (page 64).

------- Addiction: Our Responsibility --------

We can't control drink because of our body.
We can't quit and stay quit because of our mind.
Truly—no choice!
Truly—no Power!
It is not my fault.
But it is my responsibility.

Step One: The Foundation of an Arch?

In the Big Book we find an architectural analogy for the first five Steps—a spiritual arch through which we'll walk to a new freedom:

- With Step Two, we lay a "cornerstone" of willingness (page 47).
- With Step Three, we set a "keystone": we choose a new relationship with that Power (page 62).
- With Step Five, "we are building an arch through which we shall walk . . . free . . . at last" (page 75).

Isn't any arch built on a foundation? In the Twelve and Twelve discussion of Step One, we see the phrases "firm bedrock," "complete defeat," "admission of hopelessness," and "fatal nature." These are the necessary conditions that provide a solid foundation for such an arch. This foundation is our personal experience of powerlessness, our acknowledgment of our history of "no choice"—a history that may have long been obvious to others.

When I first became aware of my drinking problem—which dated from the age of twelve—I wasn't shocked at the realization. In fact, I was stunned and baffled that I had never seen it, despite all the visible evidence: blackouts, embarrassments, jails, hospital, trouble at work and home. I was graced with an experience of a problem, not just the knowledge and understanding of it. It was a small beginning, but it was a beginning. Such a realization may seem simple. But it's not easy! Only those who have an experience of Step One will be willing to go to Step Two.

I also now know only those who have an experience of Step Two will be able to continue through the following Steps and finish Step Nine.

*"If, when you honestly want to, you find you cannot quit
entirely, or if when drinking, you have little control over the
amount you take, you are probably alcoholic."*

— [first half of Step One] BIG BOOK, page 44

. . .

*"Many of us had moral and philosophical convictions galore,
but we could not live up to them even though we would
have liked to. Neither could we reduce our self-centeredness
much by wishing or trying on our own power."*

— [second half of Step One] BIG BOOK, page 62

For my first four years of recovery, starting in 1984, I went to meetings every day and called my sponsor daily. I did all Twelve Steps in my first year, without any guidance. My autobiographical Step Four work confirmed to me that I was an alcoholic. But my true recovery had not yet begun. I now realize that the work of all the Steps, and indeed of each Step, is a process that reveals itself over time. It's like thawing out. In those first four years of basic action, I thawed out externally. Over the next eight years, by submitting to the Big Book's Step work, I thawed out internally.

Starting in 1988, I engaged a guide for my Step work, a man who shared his own disciplined approach to the Big Book as a textbook. With his partnership, I learned to pray for guidance, daily and each time I sat to do the Step work; to read carefully, with a highlighter in hand; to reflect, turning statements into questions; to write as I responded to the questions; and to discuss each assignment with him to get the most out of it.

For me, prayer, willingness, and the help of an experienced guide were the keys for a new experience. Returning to Step One, I now read and understood the Big Book in a new way. I went on to review my whole state of being: body, mind, and will. Let me share that experience with you and offer three sets of questions to help you do the same.

What's Wrong with My Body?

In "The Doctor's Opinion," Dr. William Silkworth suggests that the alcoholic has a defective body (Big Book, page xxv). One out of ten people has this problem with alcohol: when we start drinking, we cannot stop. In my case, the facts soon became clear. My wife's problem was chronic: she lost control every time she drank any alcohol. My problem was periodic: it happened intermittently, not every time.

Writing in the 1930s, Dr. Silkworth hypothesized that we have an *allergy,* an abnormal reaction to a substance. While that word choice is questionable today, the idea still makes sense. I have an allergy to cats. When I'm exposed to cat dander, my eyes are irritated, my nose runs, I can't breathe, and I'm quite uncomfortable. I try to avoid cats.

When I take a drink, intending to have two, sometimes I'll have twenty-two. I take a drink, and then the drink takes me.

It was only after I fully understood these words in "The Doctor's Opinion" and then reviewed my personal drinking history that I had a new experience of *no choice.* Once I started, I often couldn't stop: now I was conscious of this phenomenon. Dr. Silkworth used the term *craving* to identify this experience, again, a word choice that can mislead us today. The dictionary defines it as "a desire for, the anticipation of." But in the Big Book, it means something that happens *after* we take the drink. The more I drink, the thirstier I get. It doesn't slake my thirst—it sets me on fire. The more I put alcohol on the fire, the hotter it burns.

Use the following questions to check out your personal history of any addiction, whether to substances or behaviors (process addictions).

Reflecting on My Body

In the spirit of the Set Aside prayer, reflect on your personal autobiography. In your paper or digital journal, write your responses to the following inventory for addiction as a disease of the body:

1. What is my experience with addiction? Do I have an abnormal reaction to a substance or process? (*Substance* refers to alcohol, other drugs, or food; *process* refers to behaviors such as compulsive gambling or sex.)

2. What happens when I indulge in this substance or process? Do I lose control once I start? List three examples.

3. What is my history of attempts to deal with it? Do I lose control every time or periodically? List five examples.

4. How successful have I been? Am I able to stop after I start? Every time? Sometimes? Hardly ever?

5. Is my use of a substance or process creating physical, emotional, social, or financial suffering for me or others?

6. With myself and with others, how honest have I been about my efforts and failures?

In 1988 I finished all the Step work, One through Twelve, and had a spiritual awakening. Within a year, I realized that I had been changed—radically.

This is a process. I'd had only a limited experience of this Step One truth: *I have an allergy of the body that produces this phenomenon of craving*, although I did not realize it was limited at the time. That limitation did not get in the way of a very transformative experience.

What's Wrong with My Mind?

In 1991, in meditation, I became aware that the "wee small voice" was inviting me to continue the journey. I engaged a new Step guide to help me, starting with Step One. With one question that guide allowed me to experience the deficiency of my mind. The question was very simple: When you have problems with alcohol, why not just stop or moderate your drinking?

Good question. Aren't some substance problems easy to address? For example, at age thirty, I had developed an allergy to thin-skinned fresh fruit. I first realized it when I ate a fig and had a strong reaction: my eyes swelled shut, I couldn't breathe, I felt extremely physically irritated, and I threw up. The next week I tried again, but first washed the fig thoroughly. I had the very same reaction. I concluded immediately that I had an allergy, and I have not eaten thin-skinned fresh fruit since. And I did not go to Figs Anonymous.

Bill W. poses a similar question in the Big Book (page 23) — why not just stop? Over the next twenty pages, his answer is revealed. He speculates that as alcoholics we have an unhealthy mind—that it is subject to an obsession that is a delusion—that we have *no choice.*

An obsession is an idea or thought that dominates our awareness in such a way that it is the only thought; it crowds out all others. Because it's our only thought, we are unaware that it's our only thought—because it is the *only* thought. It takes possession of us without our permission and without our consciousness.

The problem with this obsessive thought is that its content is a delusion. An illusion is a lie, misrepresenting reality *outside* our self. On a hot, dry day, if we see a puddle on the parking lot, it is likely a mirage. A delusion is a lie, a misrepresentation of reality *within* our self.

The Big Book refers to this as "insanity," a word from the Latin *sanus,* meaning health; in-*sanus* means *not healthy.* The Big Book's definition is " . . . lack of proportion, of the ability to think straight . . ." (page 37). "Insanity" is technically not a psychiatric disorder. It is the peculiar inability of the alcoholic (all addicts) to process reality correctly. The alcoholic or addict really believes, "It will be different this time, perhaps even better."

I don't know that I don't know; I can't see that I can't see. It's not my fault. I'm built that way. However, it is my responsibility.

My new Step guide patiently helped me review my own drinking history. The key questions were the following:

- Had I ever stopped drinking, for a period of time, and started drinking again?
- If so, what was I thinking, feeling, conscious of, or aware of *just before* I picked up the first drink after a period of abstinence?

He knew that I had not had the actual experience, i.e., conscious awareness of obsession and delusion. He did not tell me about his experience. He asked me questions based on his experience so I could be led to have my own experience. These are contained in the next set of questions.

I understood the words. I read and articulated the meanings of Jim's story and Fred's story in chapter 3 of the Big Book, discussing their similarities and differences. But I did not yet connect this information to my own experience of abstaining for a while, then drinking again. But later, as I reviewed my answers to these questions, all of a sudden there was an explosion in my consciousness: *Oh my god!* I thought. *When I started drinking again, I was not changing my mind, making a decision. I was compulsed without any consciousness at all, without any resistance at all, to begin drinking. I had no thought of why I had quit. No memory of negative consequences. No awareness at all. I just started!* I understood the "strange mental blank spot" noted in "Fred's Story" (Big Book, page 42).

Now it's your turn to think about those questions.

Reflecting on My Mind

In the spirit of the Set Aside prayer, ask yourself, reflect, and then write your responses to these questions about the disease of the mind:

1. In the past, have I made a resolution to stop a specific behavior or start a specific behavior?

2. Have I broken that resolution? If so, what did I think or feel just before I did so? Was there any premeditation? Or was I into it before I realized it?

3. How soon did I realize that I was breaking the resolution?

4. How did that make me feel?

5. Did I make another or a stronger resolution to stop (start)?

6. How well did it work? How successful have I been in stopping and staying stopped? Have there been multiple attempts?

7. How honest have I been, with others and with myself, about my efforts and my failures?

This is a process. Again, I had only a limited grasp of this new Step One truth: *I am subject to an obsession of the mind, which is a delusion (a lie I believe to be the truth)*. But again, I was not aware of the limitation. I had no clue about the meaning of unmanageability. Yet, despite this limitation, I still had a new, life-changing experience with this Step work—a broader and deeper awakening and change.

What's Wrong with My Will?

Yes, my Step One experience was definitely a process—it unfolded over ten years. The thawing continues.

In 1994, again as the result of my daily consistent prayer and meditation practice, I heard the invitation of the Spirit to find and engage another Step guide and submit to the Step work. This time, it was different: I was not coming from pain but from the awareness that more growth in consciousness was available and desirable.

During meditation, I intuited who my new guide might be. For three months I resisted: I thought he didn't seem to have anything I wanted, and we had nothing in common. But finally, since his was the only name being offered to me in my meditation, I submitted. He was the one who introduced me to a specific Set Aside prayer to use each morning and each time I sat to do any work. Working the Steps this time was a two-year process, very contemplative, and my most powerful experience up to that point. A clear demonstration that the Spirit knows best!

My new guide suggested that this time, I focus on the unmanageability aspect of Step One. Lack of power is my dilemma; my inner resources as marshaled by my will were not sufficient (Big Book, page 45). This focus was going to be on my defective will. This defect is not unique to addicts—it may be the human condition. Maybe that's why the foreword to the very first edition of the Big Book notes that "our way of living may have its advantages to all"—that is, to all humans.

The Big Book describes what unmanageability looks like behaviorally on page 52, where we find the bedevilments. Do we feel like puppets on strings that are in somebody else's control? The Big Book further suggests that the exact nature of this malady is "selfishness—self-centeredness," the "root" of our inherent human brokenness (page 62). This exact nature of the malady is described on the same page. The conclusion: not only can we not remove it on our own power, but we cannot even reduce it much "by wishing or trying on our own power." *No choice!*

The source of unmanageability is the problem of a defective will. My will, on my own power, seems to choose only me, my interests, my self, defending and fostering my ego.

— QUESTIONS FOR REFLECTION —

Reflecting on My Will

In the spirit of the Set Aside prayer, ask, reflect, and then write in your journal your responses to the following questions. Reflect on your personal history of making decisions, and your current thinking about making "free" choices and exercising your "free" will. Apply these questions to your current life, as it is today.

1. Am I having trouble with personal relationships?
2. Can I control my emotions?
3. Am I subject to misery and depression?
4. Do I derive satisfaction from my way of life?
5. Am I, or can I be, self supporting?
6. Do I feel useless or useful?

7. Am I full of fear?

8. Am I unhappy or happy?

9. Am I able to be a real help to others? Do I care?

10. Do I regularly do what I don't want to do, and regularly not do what I want to do?

11. Do I have chronic feelings of being restless, irritable, and discontent?

12. How honest have I been, with others and with myself, about my efforts and my failures?

For me, those dozen questions completed my Step One experience of powerlessness. It had taken twelve years to sufficiently thaw out to discover the real problem.

I have been given an *experience* of no power, no choice:

- of body (allergy; craving) = biology
- of mind (obsession; delusion) = psychology
- of will (unmanageability; spiritual malady) = theology

The Big Book suggests that "liquor was but a symptom" and "bottles were only a symbol" (pages 64, 103). Our real problem is lack of Power (page 45). We have a spiritual malady.

As the result of the Step One through Nine process, the Big Book promises freedom from alcohol, from addiction—we have *recovered*, been placed in a position of neutrality. But we are never *cured*. We have a daily reprieve contingent on the maintenance of our spiritual condition, that is, a consistent practice of our *way of life*: Steps Ten, Eleven, and Twelve (pages 84–85).

Ask: *Am I convinced that my life run on self-will cannot be successful?* Write out your reflection.

Now the Big Book suggests that "we had to have God's help" (pages 60, 62). We are thrust on a desperate search for a power other than self. Will this power be Healthy Steps? Higher Self? Human Spirit? Holy Spirit? Find the words that suggest a Higher Power to you.

More is to be revealed!

. . .

Personal Commitment to Action

Take these actions to get the most out of this chapter:

- *Pray the Set Aside prayer every day.*

- *Read and reflect on the referred-to sections of the Big Book.*

- *Meditatively complete the three sets of questions reflecting on the problems of body, mind, and will, using your personal history.*

- *Read the three completed sets of questions to someone who has experienced Step One.*

- *Pray for a new realization of hopelessness, doom, desperation: no choice.*

· · ·

In the next chapter, we will attempt to answer the question posed by the Big Book on page 45: Where and how are we to find this Power?

3

We Access Power through Choice

STEPS TWO AND THREE

Step Two	*Came to believe that a Power greater than ourselves could restore us to sanity.*
Step Three	*Made a decision to turn our will and our lives over to the care of God as we understood Him.*

To prepare for this chapter

Pray the following Set Aside prayer:

> *Please set aside my belief(s), my knowledge, my experiences, my feelings, my expectations about God, Higher Power, and Spirit. Allow me to have a fresh experience!*

Keep these questions in mind

- Is God or a Higher Power necessary?
- Where and how are we to find this Power?
- Is this Power a caring Reality?
- Is a relationship with this Power necessary and possible?
- How do I establish this relationship?
- What is the nature of faith?
- What is the process of choice?
- What does it mean "to turn our will and our lives over"?

Is "lack of power . . . our dilemma"?
— BIG BOOK, page 45

STEP TWO IS A DECISION *about* power—establishing our *concept* of a power greater than self. Step Three is a decision *for* power—establishing our *relationship* with that power.

The foundation to a spiritual practice of Step Eleven is the understanding, embracing, and experience of Steps Two and Three. This gives the practice focus, value, purpose, and meaning: "to improve my conscious contact". . . to be *empowered*.

I once talked with a twenty-four-year-old man who had previously been in eight treatment centers for drug and alcohol addiction. From our discussion, it was clear to me that he was now connected to recovery for the first time in a substantial way. I said so to him and asked what happened to make it different this time.

He replied, "I got tired of suffering and wanted the madness to stop."

I asked, then what? He responded, "I quit resisting."

Again, I asked, then what? He answered, "I was willing to take direction from people who wanted to help me."

He had cracked the formula for recovery. It may also be the formula to unlock the mystery of personal spirituality. Somewhere down deep inside our self is the power of choice, free will, the capacity to make a totally independent decision. It is *not* a decision about our substance or process addiction—our experience shows us that we have *no choice*: when it is in us or when it is not. It is *not* a decision about our willpower to know or do better. We have experienced that knowledge and willpower; knowing more or trying harder to do better does not work. It appears that we have little or *no choice*. My will on its own power seems capable only of choosing me—consciously, but mostly unconsciously.

In Step One, we saw that:

- we have no freedom of choice with respect to our addiction—once we start we cannot stop (body); once we stop we cannot stay stopped (mind). *No choice!*

- we have no freedom of choice with respect to our managing of our life on our own power (will)—we do what we don't want to do and we don't do what we want to do: our actual lived experience is that our lives are unmanageable, even after the gift of freedom from our addiction. My will always chooses me—a fundamental, existential survival mechanism—automatic reaction/response on my own power. *No choice!*

Have you experienced that selfishness, self-centeredness, is the root of your problem?

Our actual experience of no effective personal power leaves us in a crisis, a desperation to find a *Power* that will solve our problem, our lack of power. Our free will may be compromised by a number of influences: our genetics and family of origin, our personality, our culture, our early childhood experiences, our education, and our later life circumstances.

These influences may mitigate and dilute our real freedom of choice—but underneath it all, in the final evaluation, we are responsible for the decisions we make and the actions we take.

A major area of freedom of the will, and the component that underlies all spirituality, is the freedom to choose the God of our understanding—or no God at all. And, if we choose a God of our understanding, we also choose our relationship with *It*.

Somewhere deep down inside our self, we know we have some power of choice. We do have basic freedom of decision. This is what makes us human, responsible, and subject to shared principles and civil laws, the real basis of any civilization. We begin to wake up and hope against hope that this is true: that we have a choice and that there is a Power greater than self. Our choice is about this Power: what do I need; what do I want? Our choice is to form a relationship with this Larger Reality—what relationship have we been yearning for?

Once we begin to wake up, we begin to realize we have been asleep, and that we now have an invitation to wake up, to stay awake, and to become more awake. We also experience that we have a natural tendency to revert to being asleep. We are reminded of the dimmer switch: slowly clicking forward or backward in direct relation to our action or inaction.

When we accept the need and value for being and staying awake, we make a decision to foster a new relationship with this Reality. We accept the invitation to practice what I call Intentional Consciousness.

This choice about the nature of this Larger Reality and our decision for a relationship with *It* flows organically from our personal experience of brokenness. We make the faith decision,

— — — — — — Awakening: "Came to Believe . . ." — — — — — —

Our life is a process, not an event.

    We awaken to the Truth—we attain knowledge.

    We trust in the Love—we make a decision.

    We transmit the Spirit—we take action.

We lean into *It*; gently pressed up against *It*;
                        and realize we are *It*.

— —

hold the resulting hope, and commit to the practice of trust—trusting that *It is* and that a relationship with *It* is possible.

Explore some definitions

Five key words in the discussion of Steps Two and Three are listed here. Reflect on the meanings of these words; define them for yourself and write them in your journal for this book. For more precision and clarity, use a dictionary, if you wish.

- faith
- belief
- trust
- decision
- choice

I recommend rereading the Big Book's chapter 4, "We Agnostics," for help in considering these words. Understanding these words allowed me to apply this process to precipitate a new experience of " . . . came to believe."

— QUESTIONS FOR REFLECTION —

Believing and Behaving

With the attitude and spirit of the Set Aside prayer, reflect on these questions and then write your thoughts in your journal for this book—with all the humility and honesty you can muster.

1. What do I *actually* believe about God, Higher Power, Reality, Universe, Energy, Source, Force, Nature, Mystery, (your word)? Not my knowledge, feelings, expectations, desires; not what I've been taught, read about, been told. What do I actually believe?

2. In light of my answer to question 1, how do I actually behave? Do I trust Life? Do I behave as if there are guiding principles such as honesty, integrity, kindness, personal responsibility, humility, simplicity, compassion? Do I have a regular practice of improving my consciousness and seeking guidance from within? Is my actual behavior consistent with what I believe I believe?

At ten years of sobriety, these two questions blew my cover. I realized that I was, in practical terms, an agnostic. I thought I believed, but I did not behave as if I believed. I was awakened to my delusion. I discovered that my concept of God was the very impediment to my relationship with the Mystery.

The direction to be willing to embrace the prayer attitude of Set Aside; the reflective, deep experience of bedevilments; and the veil-rending meditation questions of belief versus behave, had challenged me and brought me to a *tabula rasa*—a clean slate, an empty white board for a new approach to "came to believe. . . ." I began to see it as a process, not an event—a process that might take a long time, but that has a very distinct methodology and transformative impact. Again, it's like a dimmer switch: click, click, click . . . the incremental brightness lets me see what I couldn't before.

Do you fully accept that there is not an adequate word for this Reality? If *It* is, *It* is infinite—with no beginning or end. Since we are finite and material, we use words that are finite and material—totally inadequate to contain the reality of Infinite/Immaterial. But as humans we need words, metaphors, similes, symbols, poetry, and even some logic to express ourselves. Just realize that when it comes to *It*—there are no adequate words. The ocean cannot be contained in a bucket!

So the Big Book asks us a question on page 47: "Do you believe?" And if you don't yet: "Are you willing to believe?" The assumption is that the reader has had a real experience of *no personal power*—perhaps through some aspect of addiction (the first half of Step One) or of the bedevilments, the spiritual malady, of unmanageability (the second half of Step One). Thus, the assumption is that the experience of no personal power has produced a disposition of openness and even a desperate need for some kind of power to stay abstinent at the least, and to live life comfortably at the most.

The Big Book's question is gentle, with a fallback position: Are you at least willing to believe? The Big Book suggests this is the cornerstone for the spiritual arch that leads to freedom (page 47). After some more poetry, logic, science, and outright cajoling, we arrive at a much more black-and-white question, not so gentle: "God is or God isn't; God is Everything or God is nothing; *What is your choice?*" (page 53). Very confrontational!

So what exactly is faith? Not certitude or knowledge; not feeling or emotion. Faith is not a function of the head (thought) or the body (feelings). Perhaps faith is simply a choice, a decision of our *free* will. There is no absolute certitude; there is no felt feeling. We make a choice out of pure desperation. We're totally hopeless if we don't choose: there is a Power other than mine, other than human.

I do not know what *It* is. I cannot put *It* into adequate words. I don't necessarily have any positive feelings about *It*. I just choose! My choice is: *It* is. There is a Power. It may be Nature, a Source, a Force, an Energy, a Reality, a Creator of all that is—I don't, and can't, know for sure.

Now here is the alchemic magic. I have made a decision—that is my act of faith, my free choice. There is no evidence ("the evidence of things not seen"). But my mind, viewing this decision, accepts it as true—because if it's not true, all is lost. My mind concludes that it's reasonable. My mind's acceptance of this faith decision thus becomes my belief. Then the rubber meets the road. My body translates both the faith decision and the belief tenet as true: I act "as if" this expresses reality. I behave as if what I decided and believe is true—this is my act of trust.

There is no substance to faith; it is dark, thin—merely a decision. Richard Rohr says that faith is the acceptance of a Reality without any evidence, and once we accept it, the evidence for that Reality begins to appear!

Spiritual alchemy: the iron of doubt has been converted to the gold of action. I live "as if" and my life works. Perhaps that is evidence enough.

The silver bullet of Step Two is the open, all-inclusive invitation to choose our own concept. Twelve Step programs have no dogma to believe; they have a few suggestions about what to do.

Choose your own concept! What word or phrase captures the qualities or attributes you need *It* to be or to have now, at this time? Your needs and concept will change over time. "Came to believe" is a process. Gandhi suggested that our concept of God will change as we do.

Ask, reflect, choose, and write in your journal the qualities and attributes you need in your Higher Power.

This choice may involve spiritual fourth dimension vocabulary—a concept that references Holy Spirit. Or this choice may be for simply working the rest of the Steps to regain my health. Or it can be for the human spirit found in your recovery group, as the Twelve and Twelve suggests. Or the choice may be for the higher self of some psychologies or Eastern religions. Whatever we choose, we act as if our choice is based on the reality that *It* is. We make a decision that this Larger Reality is and is concretely true.

The Big Book suggests we decide that someplace deep down inside us is a sufficient Power (page 53). I choose, with all the power of my free will, that "an unsuspected inner resource" is so (pages 567–68).

Perhaps, if *It* is, *It* is

- infinite: *It* has no beginning and no end
- unconditional: *It* has no needs, therefore, *It* is Pure Love
- unilateral: *It* offers an overflow of creative, generative action
- present: There is no place where *It* is not
- caring: *It* created me so that I might enjoy just being. What other reason could there be?

Is your choice for a caring Reality?

– – – – Love Is Action; Love Is a Relationship – – – – –

Love is giving of oneself, without conditions, so that another may be and may flourish. Love, the word, is a symbol of this action. Love is unconditional, creative. Love is an action.

Love is unconditional when the Giver has no needs, no preconditions, just overflows Itself. Its Grace is unearned and ever-present. It is life that cannot be gained by action— life that cannot be lost by action.

It is creative because the gift is existence. Before me there was *It* and only *It*—without beginning. I find my beginning in *It*—an overflow of generosity: I am not *It*; but I am not *not It*.

Love is a relationship because *It* is dynamic. Its nature is goodness generating goodness—the innate movement of the Unmoved Mover.

And Love *loving* is a relationship.

– –

Step Two is a thought-filled decision *about* God—a meditation. Step Three is a yearning-filled decision *for* a relationship with a caring God—a prayer. Again, this is our choice, a selection by our free will, a decision.

Am I convinced by my experiences that there is no sufficient power in me, that *is* me? Have I made a decision, a choice that there is a Power, deep down within me, that is available to me?

Now the question is, how do we access that Power? We are invited to again make a decision, a choice using the inherent power of our free will. The decision is "to turn" our will and our life over to the *care* of God. Note: not "to God" but to the "care of God"!

Step Three is not passive. (The word *surrender* does not appear in the original first 164 pages of the Big Book.) What does it mean "to turn"? Perhaps it means to align ourselves with Reality; to turn from our natural inclination to be self-centered; to gradually become other-centered. Could this be what is meant by the terms *spiritual malady* and *spiritual awakening*, respectively?

Is there a unilateral flow of the Source of Reality? Is not our "turning" a ferocious act of my free choice to be in alignment with that flow of Love manifesting as life, as the universe, as me as I really am?

What is "our will and our life"? Could it be . . .

- our power of choice and the actions that follow?
- who we are and what we have?
- our decisions to take action and the consequences of these actions?

And again, is powerlessness our experience? Can we even reduce our self-centeredness much by wishing or trying on our own power? The Big Book suggests not (page 62). Being convinced we cannot: "we stood at the turning point" (page 59).

Bill W. had summarized it earlier in his own story, told in the Big Book: "Simple but not easy; a price had to be paid. It meant destruction of self-centeredness. I must *turn* in all things to the Father of Light who presides over us all" (page 14; italics added).

Being convinced of our need for Power, we decide to expand our decision *about* Power to a decision *for* Power, for a relationship with Power. The Big Book suggests this is the keystone to the spiritual arch introduced in Step Two. This decision holds the entire spiritual arch together—an arch through which we can pass to freedom: freedom from addiction, freedom from the spiritual malady.

The Big Book describes the promises of Step Three: "We had a new Employer. Being all powerful, He provided what we needed [note: not *wanted*], if we kept close to Him and performed His work well. Established on such a footing, we became less and less interested in ourselves, our little plans and designs. More and more we became interested in seeing what we could contribute to life. As we felt new power flow in, as we enjoyed peace of mind, as we discovered we could face life successfully, as we became conscious of His presence, we began to lose our fear of today, tomorrow or the hereafter. We were reborn" (page 63).

These promises represent Steps Two and Three as a process, not an event; an experience, not a task; a beginning, not an end. Steps Two and Three are a decision expressed in prayer, not an action but the promise of action, to be voiced without reservation at the same time we humbly realize we are powerless to do so.

What "relationship" do you want . . . do you *yearn* for? The Big Book suggests some options for names for a Higher Power: Director, Principal, Father, Employer, Maker/Creator. Some people choose words such as Mother, Lover, Healer, Teacher/Mentor,

Friend/Companion, Source, Force, Energy, or Nature. (Or, as we noted earlier, Healthy Steps, Higher Self, Human Self, Holy Spirit.)

Currently my choice is Mystery. For me, *It* is unknowable. I choose to believe that *It* is and that my journey is to improve my conscious contact by gently leaning on and into *It*. I consent to *It* drawing me forward in my organic, spiritual evolution. I give *It* explicit permission to have *Its* way with me. This is my choice!

The Step Three prayer wording is optional—prayer is an intention, not a string of words.

———————— We Awaken to Compassion ————————

Love is God.
Loving is us.
Are we the image and likeness?
To know who we are—image?
To be who we are—likeness?
It is a very slow process of awakening:
Waking up to the delusion of twoness,
Living as the reality of oneness,
Until we become aware of the reality of unity.

Meanwhile we foster it:
    With all our mind,
    With all our heart,
    With all our strength.

And we do this through conscious acts of anonymous helping; in the beginning contrary to our inclination; over time, organically becoming devoted to compassionate service; one with Love Loving.

———————————————————————————

Circumstances made me willing to believe. Desperation brought me to choose. I humbly offered to align myself with my understanding of the flow of Life—to turn from self-centeredness to Life-Centeredness. To be in harmony, to be in synchrony with human and universal principles, to row with the flow.

I intend to express this idea without reservation and simultaneously realize humbly the impossibility of doing that. I have reservations. I am willing to turn, with the full faith expectation that I will be turned. My willingness will activate Grace; Grace will activate my willingness.

Thomas Merton suggests that God is that Reality that has no circumference and whose center is everywhere. The Big Book speaks similarly about this Reality.

- *It is transcendent*:
  We "must turn in all things to the Father of Light who presides over us all" (page 14).

- *It is immanent*:
  ". . . Spirit of the Universe underlying the totality of things" (page 46).

What do you want and need to believe? What do you want and need as a relationship?

What do you decide to believe? What do you decide to have as a relationship?

You choose!

• • •

Personal Commitment to Action

Make a commitment to your own Larger Reality.

- *Choose a concept of Power — your concept.*
- *Choose the relationship you yearn to have—your choice.*
- *Write out an intention of alignment—your prayer.*

Hold yourself accountable.

- *Read this commitment to a trusted confidante.*
- *Ask this person to pray with you as a public witness to your commitment.*

. . .

4

We Awaken by Naming Obstacles to Power

STEP FOUR

Step Four	Made a searching and fearless moral inventory of ourselves.

To prepare for this chapter

Prepare for this chapter by creating your own Set Aside prayer reflecting your willingness to identify the obstacles within you that prevent a dynamic relationship with whatever you call your Creative Life Force.

Keep these questions in mind

- What are the impediments in me to a relationship with my higher or spiritual Self?
- Where do these impediments come from?
- How are they removed?
- What is the intrinsic relationship of prayer and meditation to doing an inventory?
- What is a healthy spiritual approach to doing an inventory?

*"We launched out on a course of vigorous action,
the first step of which is a personal housecleaning . . .
a strenuous effort to face, and to be rid of, the things
in ourselves which had been blocking us . . ."*

— BIG BOOK, pages 63–64

WEBSTER SUGGESTS AN inventory is "an itemized list." The Latin root of this word means "to find." Step Four indicates a "moral inventory," which means examining our actions in relationship to our guiding principles of right and wrong. It does not mean a negative judgmental evaluation of our "sins," but rather an objective observation of our *motives, values, beliefs,* and especially our *actions* and their impact on others. It may be our first attempt at seeing reality as it really is, and ourselves as we really are. This is an effort at confirming the *truth.*

We are shaped by our biology, psychology, and sociology—our culture and the people around us. Our DNA and our environment develop the lens through which we perceive and process reality. This lens alters our perceptions and ultimately our behavior, in progression like this:

Perceptions ➔ Thoughts ➔ Feelings ➔ Attitudes ➔ Behaviors

We don't know reality as *It* is; we know reality as *we* are. We have a distorted lens that creates our delusions about reality. Our suffering comes from living through these delusions. We are asleep, dreaming that we are awake. We need to wake up and stay awake.

The beginning of this path was to resolve the "no power of choice" versus "power of choice" questions in Steps One, Two, and Three. Now, using prayer and meditation, we approach the Step Four inventory to improve our sight and insight.

Inventory goes hand-in-glove with Intentional Consciousness (prayer and meditation). Which brings us to a key question with multiple parts: What are the specific prayers in the Big Book to facilitate the effectiveness of Step Four? We have prayers that help us

- identify and analyze all resentments
- remove deep resentments
- recognize, reduce, and remove our fears
- guide us to implement spiritual principles with respect to our sexual behavior
- deal with dishonesty and secrets

Hopefully we have experienced that we are powerless—we are not effective on our own power. Our personal history of serial suffering, as revealed in Step One, has demonstrated that fact, not just with respect to our addiction(s) but also with regard to our living a quality life.

Thus begins our desperate and deliberate search for an effective relationship with Power in Steps Two and Three. We decided there is a Power; *It* is deep down inside me. I decided I can have a relationship with *It*—deep down inside me. Ask yourself: Do I have it? If not, why not? Perhaps because the Sunlight in me is blocked by the clouds in me. These clouds need to be identified and removed.

Step Four names the underlying causes and conditions, the exact nature of these obstacles. Steps Five through Nine dissipate and even remove them. Step Ten is the personal inventory tool suggested to remove them on the spot whenever we're disturbed. Step Eleven provides the means (Intentional Consciousness) to effectively do an evening inventory as part of our meditation practice, a review to pick up and deal with those disturbances we missed during our active day.

We will never transcend our humanity. We will constantly revert to our self-centeredness. But we have a perennial organic invitation from a Power greater than ourselves to restore our humanity. We make a daily effort to repent (turn) and reform (change) through Intentional Consciousness—co-creating our life through Grace and willingness.

I turn again to my favorite metaphor for our spiritual journey—the dimmer switch. At first it clicks on at a very low voltage, producing very little light. As we turn the dial, one click at a time, it brightens very slowly. In fact, the dialing up is so subtle that we are not aware of any more light. But at some point, there is enough light to see that which we did not previously see. We stay gently pressed up against it—shoulder to the dial. It continues its slow progress forward. Finally, there is an experience of awakening—en*light*enment. There is enough Light to see.

Our life also teaches us that the dimmer switch is rigged to go backward, spring-loaded to move toward the darkness. So we need to be vigilant—to pay attention, to watch. It is a spiritual

— — — — — — — — I Am Shadow and Light — — — — — — — —

By running from our shadows, we feed our inner darkness. We reduce and eliminate our shadows by moving into and becoming light.

I am a product of Love and therefore, in my very nature, I am love. When I am true to my very nature, I am love loving.

I sit in the Light becoming light. My shadows begin to wane and then disappear. As I become Light, I am a channel of Light. Giving light to those around me helps the shadows to wane and disappear. Being a conduit of Light allows *them* to become light—to become truly who they are: Love loving.

— —

axiom: "When I am disturbed, there is something wrong with me!" (Twelve and Twelve, page 90).

We learned in Step One's "unmanageability" that "our troubles . . . are basically of our own making" (Big Book, page 62). Now, in Step Four, we are going to discover what this means and experience the spiritual malady of unmanageability in living color. Step Four is Step One in writing.

Understanding Step Four: An Overview

"Selfishness—self-centeredness . . . is the root of our troubles," says the Big Book (page 62). With the Step Four inventory, we face the fallout from these troubles. The Big Book focuses on three major areas: resentment (or anger), fear, and sex. All share the theme of dishonesty—inability or unwillingness to see, know, and admit. And all are manifested in behavior, with selfishness/self-centeredness as the root, or source.

The Twelve and Twelve suggests that our inventory is about instincts gone awry. These are our natural survival instincts: *fight, flight,* and *freeze* (seeking camouflage)—the very continued existence of the individual is dependent on them. At their basic level: anger motivates fight, fear motivates flight, and deception motivates the camouflaging "freeze" instinct (dishonesty).

These are hard-wired into our very nature. We cannot get rid of them, nor should we since they are key to our very survival. But they have become maladaptive and have developed into unhealthy habits because of our distorted addict's lens on life. We have cataracts that have grown slowly over time because of ignorance, dysfunctional environment, and our unhealthy over-reactions ("self-will run riot").

The Big Book concludes: "Neither could we reduce our self-centeredness much by wishing or trying on our own power.

We had to have God's help" (page 62). We are powerless; we need Power!

Addressing resentments

The Latin roots for our verb "to resent" are *sentire,* to feel, and *re-,* again, holding the clue to its definition: anger held and ruminated about repeatedly, nursed and inflamed. The Big Book suggests this is the number one offender as a source of spiritual disease (page 64). Resentment is not a thought, or a memory of anger. It is the current feeling of an active, lingering anger.

My Step guide suggested that when I sit to begin any work, I pray the Set Aside prayer for an open mind and heart, and that I write a spontaneous prayer at the top of each page before I begin writing. Examples: *"God, help me see my beliefs"* . . . *"Holy Spirit, please inspire me with energy to do this work"* . . . *"Higher Power, lead me to the truth."*

The Big Book suggests we make three columns on a sheet of paper (page 65). In column 1, we name what we resent: people, institutions, and principles. In column 2, we list the causes for that resentment. Then for column 3, we are asked what areas of our lives are affected, "hurt or threatened . . . interfered with?" In the Big Book's example, we see these areas listed: self-esteem, pride, ambition, security, personal relationships, sex relations, and pocketbooks.

"We searched out the flaws in our make-up which caused our failure."

— BIG BOOK, page 64

But we find no definitions of these seven areas, nor any instruction on how to apply them. They are simply listed for review in column 3. My first time through the Big Book, I treated the exercise as a check-the-box matchup and had no new *experience* as a result. The next time through the Steps, I was given definitions and specific instructions for analysis. I was able to see the lens through which I'd been looking. I was given the gift of identifying my delusional beliefs, corrupt motives, and ignored values. (Note: Details can be found in my book *Twelve Steps to Spiritual Awakening,* and a column 3 worksheet is contained in the "Our Way of Life" document downloadable from the Herb K. website: www.HerbK.com.)

The point is that as a result of an overwhelmingly embarrassing *experience* of my Neanderthal delusions about myself, I was given a new connection to powerlessness, which prepared me to receive a new approach to resentments through prayer. This led to a previously unavailable freedom from my deep resentments.

My Step guide asked me to list my "deep resentments"—those whose roots reached down into my guts, my cellular structure, my very soul. Of my eighty-five resentments, eight were deep ones: father, mother, high school coach, wife, and four bosses (I had had only four bosses!).

My Big Book assignment was to read the resentment comments beginning on page 65 with the words "We went back through our lives . . ." and ending on page 67 with " . . . to take a kindly and tolerant view of each and every one." The purpose of this assignment was

1. to locate the deep resentments that were still in me even after two prior Step Four efforts
2. to realize that I was powerless over them: identifying, analyzing, and confessing did not remove them. "We

could not wish them away any more than alcohol" (page 66). *No choice!*

3. to follow the Big Book's prayer practice to remove these deep resentments—which is the "key to our future" (pages 67–68).

We need to look at these resentments from "an entirely different angle," says the Big Book. They can really dominate us and cause suffering, to us and to the people we resent. We need to set aside our hurt and begin to think of these people who objectively harmed us as "spiritually sick"—no longer taking it all personally. We, too, are spiritually sick, just like everybody else. We adopt compassion for them and humility for ourselves.

The spiritual cancer of anger seriously diminishes the quality of my life, but I am powerless to remove it. Thus, I learned, I need to pray for the removal of this resentment.

How do I pray? I ask God to help me show the person tolerance, compassion, and patience. I ask how to be helpful. I ask for freedom from this specific resentment. Praying this way, I am actually praying for myself. I am *not* praying for them! *I am praying for me,* for my healing, for my freedom. I trust that God will show me how to take a kindly and tolerant view of this person, institution, principle, or circumstance.

My Step guide asked me to create a personal prayer that would express the idea and the spirit of removing these specific resentments. I was to pray my prayer each day—one for the removal of each specific resentment. (See the prayer that follows.)

I began this suggested prayer practice. In three months of consistent daily prayer for the removal of each of my eight deep resentments, nothing happened. Then one day I realized that I had no negative energy for one of the deep ones. I crossed it off

In this prayer, insert the name of the person involved with your resentment.

> God, _____ [name], like me, is a spiritually sick person. Please help me to show _____ [name] tolerance, compassion, and patience. Please forgive me for being angry and enable me to stop clinging to this resentment. Please remove this resentment and show me how to take a kindly and tolerant view of _____ [name]. Please show me how I can be helpful to _____ [name]. Thy will be done!

my list. Over the next several weeks of consistent daily prayer, the list melted away like snow in spring. They were all removed.

The miracle of this prayer process and practice is that the next time I did a Step Four inventory, three years later, there was no trace of the prior resentments. In fact, I had a difficult time identifying *any* resentments.

But we never transcend our humanity. This time my new Step guide suggested I look at "who's annoying or irritating me." I developed a list!

The final phase of the resentment inventory is described in the Big Book on page 67, second full paragraph. Again, it is suggesting *setting aside*, "putting out of our minds the wrongs others had done . . . [disregarding] the other person involved entirely."

In the spirit of prayer and discernment through meditation, we look for our own mistakes, self-seeking, blame, faults, wrongs. We look at our responsibility—not at actions of others or the impacts of circumstances on us, but our reaction to those actions and impacts. We have very little responsibility or even influence over the actions of others or the impact of circumstances. We have

100 percent responsibility for our reaction to them. Whose reaction is it? Whose feelings are these? Who is responsible for my reactions and my feelings?

I am—but only 100 percent of the time! I do not have a part; I have 100 percent of the whole.

Welcome to emotional sobriety. This is what it means to be an adult, to be response-able. This shift cuts the puppet strings of codependency and allows me to begin to become independent instead of dependent. You cannot name me. Nor can my mistakes name me. I keep my center of gravity inside myself, not in you. Eventually, this allows me to realize the healing effect of the process of forgiveness—a decision to release, which in turn releases me. The spiritual paradox:

- When I admit powerlessness, I am empowered.
- When I take responsibility, I am set free.
- When I bring healing, I am healed.

We have begun a rite of passage that deconstructs our fabricated self and reveals our true self—to ourselves and then to the community that surrounds and supports our journey.

Addressing fear

How do we address our fear? Not the thought or memory of fear, but any current feelings of fear, anxiety, worry, or dread?

The Big Book is very straightforward here: Put your fears on paper. Name them. Make a list. Then ask yourself and write out the answer: Why do I have this fear?

Again, my Step guide suggested that when I begin to do any inventory work I pray the Set Aside prayer; that I write a spontaneous prayer at the top of each page asking for help to identify underlying causes and conditions, to see the destructive patterns of my fears, to be brought to release from fear through trust in the Source of Power.

My guide also took an analytical approach. He suggested I keep questioning each iteration of my answer. *Why is that so? What will take place if that happens?* This is a prayerful search for the exact nature of my fears, a meditation to determine the underlying causes and conditions of this specific fear.

He indicated we are born with only two natural fears: fear of falling, and fear of loud noises. All other fears are learned.

The Big Book suggests that the ultimate answer to the question about the source of fear is our tendency toward self-reliance. We know intuitively that we are finite, not smart enough, not powerful enough, not fast enough to survive on our own power. Our personal history of actual experiences supports this notion.

There is a better way, says the Big Book: relying upon the God of our understanding. We made this decision in Step Three, turning our life and will over to the *care* of God. We need to answer the question about our purpose: What is our role? If we figure this out, make a decision of *faith* to believe, then make a decision of trust to act as if what we believe is true, and then rely on this Power greater than self, we'll find serenity: a sense of purpose, meaning, and value. Even if we can name our fears, describe and understand their sources, we are powerless to actually remove them. So we pray for their removal. The Big Book suggests we will begin to outgrow fear (page 68).

Addressing sex

About sexual matters, the Big Book implores us to be sensible, use common sense, take the middle path, and, above all, get guidance (pages 68–70).

Again, we are to make a list. This time the Big Book provides a specific list of questions to be asked (page 69). The Big Book is quite clear: Alcoholics Anonymous has no opinion—but each of us does. With this process we discover the truth about our own principles, values, beliefs —we are individually responsible for knowing and behaving in accordance with them.

Again my Step guide suggested I write a prayer at the top of each page asking for an open mind and heart—for revelation of the truth.

I asked for guidance so that when I answered each question, I would see the pattern of my selfishness and insensitivity, to become aware of the hurt I inflicted on others, directly and indirectly. This was a process of reflection, using my mind to think on the intention of prayer.

The most powerful question for me in the list on page 69 was " . . . what should we have done instead?"

When, in prayer, I honestly asked myself about my current consciousness with respect to past sexual conduct, I found guidelines for treating myself and others. I wish to be honest, to view others as friends, to be considerate, to have integrity and faithfulness, and to think of others' needs and happiness as well as my own.

Through this question-and-answer process, the principles deep inside of me—my principles—were revealed and became the grist for the mill to the development of my personal sexual values. These became the guidelines for current and future behavior. As the Big Book puts it (page 69), "In meditation, we ask God" first, for knowledge of these principles and ideals; second, for the power to carry them out, to "help us to live up to them." We pray for guidance on what we should do—knowledge for our mind and the willingness/strength to grow toward these principles—power for our will.

Contemporary perspectives on sex

The Big Book sex inventory is not about sexual conduct itself. It is about our motives and our behavior's impact on others. It helps us identify our attitudes, feelings, and thinking at the root of our behavior. It suggests we inventory our history of actual awareness and behavior, that we consider what we *should have done instead*. Then we use our answers to:

- identify the desired operating principles that will guide our future healthy behavior.

- confer with others for more information or experience to help us determine what "healthy" might mean.

- pray and meditate to receive guidance and come to some conclusion about our future personal sex conduct.

Again, each individual is responsible for their own thinking, feeling, attitude, and behavior. Of course, the entire inventory discussion assumes voluntary decisions and behaviors that are based on personal choice and mutual participation.

The Big Book was written in an era and culture quite different from our own. Much has changed in social and psychological awareness, education, and cultural standards. We are now much more informed and aware of the number of human deviations and dysfunctions connected to human sexual energies:

- sexual abuse, incest, molestation, and rape of both female and male children

- trauma and related PTSD coming from people's (especially women's) experiences with physical and sexual abuse, prostitution, and sex trafficking

- the emerging awareness of love addiction, relationship addiction, and sex addictions, including Internet pornography

- the emotional turmoil that is part and parcel of the trauma of the prejudice, rejection, and abuse around differences in sexual orientation and preferences
- the dysfunctional guilt and shame brought on by all these activities

For many, the impacts of this extensive and broadening world of hurt can be devastating psychologically. Remember, the sex inventory is intended to address the person's motives and behavior of sex activities that come from that person's choice. Although one's personal history is definitely material for Steps Four and Five and, later, Eight and Nine, the Step process will not be, nor can it be, adequate to address and resolve many of these issues.

Dr. John Wellwood says the belief that spirituality can fix all psychological problems is false and names that belief "spiritual bypass." [4] In many cases involving the above traumatic issues, professional intervention and treatment will be absolutely necessary to bring about an individual's healing and wholeness.

Further comment is beyond the scope of this book. Fortunately, a variety of resources are widely available to those who need professional expertise.

Some additional Step Four inventory topics

The Big Book's three topics of inventory—resentment, fear, and sex—are quite comprehensive. But some extra reflections might make your Step Four experience—and the Step Five experience to follow—more complete.

Remember that the purpose of this process is to identify and remove (*have* removed) the impediments and obstacles to a relationship with Power deep down inside us. After praying the Set Aside prayer, spend time reflecting or meditating on these additional items listed below and write out your thoughts, feelings, and memories.

In the spirit of Set Aside, ask yourself where and when you have experienced these:

- dishonesty (including stealing)
- secrets
- embarrassment
- irresponsibility: financial, relationship, behavior, family, work
- guilt—an unhealthy feeling toward my history of behavior
- shame—an unhealthy feeling toward my very being as a person

Consider if you want to look at violations of moral principles (values) as expressed in the seven capital sins as suggested in Step Four in the Twelve and Twelve:

- pride
- greed
- lust
- gluttony
- envy
- anger
- sloth

Be specific. It is especially important to be specific about any area or item that you have resistance to. Err on the side of maximizing rather than minimizing. This is about rigorous honesty and about being transparent. This is about removing sludge in us that blocks us from God. This is about cleaning the channel of and for Intentional Consciousness.

Ask yourself: How free do I want to be?

This is the pilgrim's journey: a passage from the way of the child, self-centered and self-obsessed; a passage to other-centeredness: a relationship with the source of Power, the Spirit of the Universe underlying the totality of things; a relationship with our community of human beings with whom we share this journey.

Wisdom is seeing as God sees and living in harmony with God's will: We take responsibility for our thoughts, our feelings, our behavior, our lives. We invite the wisdom-spirit to enter our lives:

- to change our loneliness into our solitude.
- to change our outward-reaching into our inward-search.
- to change our fearful clinging into fearless service.

Underneath all is abiding, creative energy. Everything is a manifestation of this creative energy. We are the image and likeness. We are knowledge and action. We are Mind and Spirit. We are a holy community. We are a Fellowship of the Spirit.

———————————————————————————————————

Inventory of our consciousness practices

It is suggested that as food, water, air, and sunshine are vital for sustaining our physical life, prayer and meditation are vital for nourishing our spiritual life. Trappist monk Thomas Merton suggested that meditation is the combustion chamber of the false self. Philosopher of spirituality Ken Wilber and psychiatrist Daniel Siegel both suggest that the consistent daily practice of prayer and meditation elevates consciousness by at least two levels and even changes our brain's neuron synapses, creating new thought patterns and therefore new behaviors and habits through *right thinking*.[5]

Personal Reflection

Completing an inventory is essential to having an effective meditation practice. Prayer and meditation are essential for the completion of a Step Four inventory. They are hand-in-glove. Therefore, reexamine what you took from chapter 1 on prayer and meditation by answering the following questions:

- *What is prayer? Do I pray? Why do I or don't I?*
- *What is meditation?*
- *Do I believe meditation is important? Do I do it? Am I consistent?*
- *Why and how do I meditate? Or don't I?*
- *How do I handle distractions? Do I inventory the sources of my distractions?*
- *How do I know I'm doing it correctly? Has my behavior improved?*
- *Do I want to pray and meditate? Do I want to have "improved consciousness"?*
- *Really?*

. . .

Now, let's explore the view and final phase of the work of soul surgery of the self rendered through Steps Five, Six, and Seven.

5

We Continue Awakening by Establishing a Healthy Self

STEPS FIVE, SIX, AND SEVEN

Step Five	*Admitted to God, to ourselves, and to another human being the exact nature of our wrongs.*
Step Six	*Were entirely ready to have God remove all these defects of character.*
Step Seven	*Humbly asked Him to remove our shortcomings.*

To prepare for this chapter

Prepare by praying the following Set Aside prayer:

Please, _____ [name your Power], bring to my awareness the obstacles in me that are the impediments to my relationship with Reality, and grant me willingness to cooperate and take the actions to have them removed.

Keep these questions in mind

What am I actually willing to do?

- Open discussion of my entire inventory?
- Reveal all secrets?
- Be willing to change my behavior?
- Pray for removal of specific defects of character?
- Be held accountable for these specific behaviors?
- Create my vision of my true self?

"Certain defects . . . weak items in our personal inventory . . .
are about to be cast out."

— BIG BOOK, page 72

STEPS FIVE, SIX, AND SEVEN take us through the next phase in the process of "turning": *revelation* and *reformation*.

We share our inventory, holding back nothing. Our goal is total transparency. We pray for sight (Intentional Consciousness) and strength. At the conclusion of the reading of the inventory, we once again are invited to a process of prayer and meditation. We cannot do this on our own—we are powerless to see and to name the whole truth about our self. Then, in prayer, we name our defects of character that have developed from a life of habitual "self-will run riot." We see, once again, that even though we know better, we do not do better.

We realize we need power other than from our self and are again invited to pray "My Creator . . ." to be re-created.

Step Five

Approach Step Five with the Set Aside spirit: We suspect that we are neither fully informed about "the exact nature of our wrongs," nor 100 percent willing to reveal them at full depth to another human being. We may feel a certain powerlessness to know, or to even be willing to know. This powerlessness may extend to our reluctance to tell on ourselves and reveal our extensive embarrassing history of selfishness and self-centeredness.

We may have grown up in a religious tradition that used confession. We may have had some experience with professional therapy. We may even have done previous Step Five work. Even so, this upcoming suggested Step Five process may still be somewhat intimidating. But the Big Book authors knew this and laid out the ultimate value proposition for doing it: "If we skip this vital step, we may not overcome drinking" (page 72).

It is to be a "humbling experience." That is the point Bill W. made in his own story: " . . . a price had to be paid. It meant destruction of self-centeredness" (page 14). It is about the beginning of identifying and dismantling the persona that we have fabricated in our historical efforts at survival, especially emotionally. We have created a mask, a Hollywood façade, a false self to protect our true self. In the beginning, these defenses may have actually been necessary and useful. As we grow older, they become unhealthy habits of perception and behavior. They create the distorted lens, the cataracts, through which we perceive ourselves, others, and circumstances that are the sources of our suffering. We don't see reality as it is; we see reality as *we are.* Dysfunctional reactions, ours and other people's, are the inevitable result and experience.

The keys to Step Five are "humility, fearlessness, and honesty," to tell someone *all* my story (page 73). Transparency is the goal, having my inside and outside match.

When faced with this action, we intuitively know we are really powerless to do it transparently. So we pray. We also pray for guidance to select the person who is to hear our inventory. This is a meditation. We ask and then listen to the wee small voice for guidance, an intuitive thought. Most often, this person will be our sponsor or Step guide; it can be our therapist, spiritual director, minister, or trusted friend. The Big Book is very clear: we choose.

When I am asked to hear a Fifth Step, I begin by inviting the person to join me in praying the Set Aside prayer to open our hearts and minds to the movement of the Spirit. This prayer is for both of us: the person to reveal all and me to listen deeply. Step Five is not a discussion; it is mostly a monologue.

My practice is to read out loud the beginning of the Big Book's chapter 6, "Into Action," with the person, alternating paragraphs from page 72 into page 75. It's an excellent icebreaker, reducing the tension in both of us. We read something safe. We hear our own and each other's voices. We are reminded of the purpose of the process and the Big Book's suggestions for doing it. I stop on page 75 after reading the line "We pocket our pride and go to it, illuminating every twist of character, every dark cranny of the past."

The person then begins to read their inventory. When the person has finished, I read the next line on page 75: "Once we have taken this step, *withholding nothing* . . ." I ask if they've written down all their secrets; I also ask if they've read everything they wrote down. I pause. The silence creates a tension that will generally help the person cough up anything consciously withheld.

I read the Step Five promises (page 75) as the beginning of the suggested meditation. These are the expected and hoped for results of this phase of the process.

> We can look the world in the eye. We can be alone at perfect peace and ease. Our fears fall from us. We begin to feel the nearness of our Creator. We may have had certain spiritual beliefs, but now we begin to have a spiritual experience. The feeling that the drink problem has disappeared will often come strongly. We feel we are on the Broad Highway, walking hand in hand with the Spirit of the Universe.

The Big Book suggests finding a quiet place where the person can meditate for an hour. The meditation instructions are very clear:

- We start with prayer: " . . . thank God . . . that we know Him better."
- We use the Big Book as a guide for the meditative review: on page 59, Steps One through Five are listed.

- We carefully read each Step asking, "Have I omitted anything?" This is a meditation—directed thinking about our diligence and honesty.
- We make a thoughtful review of the instructions received, the actions taken, the honesty experienced.

These are the building blocks for the spiritual arch through which we walk to freedom (page 75).

- Step One: Foundation of powerlessness
- Step Two: Cornerstone of willingness to believe
- Step Three: Keystone of decision for alignment with God's will

Delusional Seeing

How we see determines *what* we see.

The ego's agenda is narcissistic self-development, protection, and survival. We reframe reality to reflect the picture we want to see. We look through the lens of our beliefs and create our reality. No wonder we have problems!

Our ego is a construct of our energies for survival:

to have life itself
to have pleasure
to have meaning

When it is focused totally on ourself, it is the construct of our false self—insuring survival but also isolation and unhappiness.

This ego is the enemy within, the "devil" that defeats us.

In the beginning, it is a natural and necessary development of our personal evolution. But later, if not transcended, it becomes a false persona that prevents the revelation of our true self. The bondage of self—our personal prison.

The truth will set you free, but first it will annoy you.

Perhaps the "stones" referred to in that final paragraph of instructions in the Big Book are the Step Four building blocks of the diagnosis of the actual problem so we can apply the suggested specific solution. The manifestations of the problem are our behavior caused by resentment, fear, inappropriate sex, dishonesty, and secrets. The root nature of the problem is "Selfishness—self-centeredness!" (page 62).

And we are powerless to deal effectively with these manifestations, or the root, so we are asked to pray. And we are even more powerless over their source, so we are asked again to pray.

Step Six

As I observed at the beginning of this book, it is because we can know and we can decide to take voluntary actions that make us human. The Steps are built to address our human nature. The *even* Steps are suggestions *to know by naming:*

Step Two:
our concept of Higher Power

Step Four:
the obstacles to a relationship with Higher Power

Step Six:
the personality disorders that come from these
maladaptive defense systems

Step Eight:
the impact of our dysfunctional behavior on others

Step Ten:
continue to name "disturbances"

Step Twelve:
name and carry message; name and practice principles

The *odd* Steps are suggestions *to decide to take specific actions:*

Step One:
admit defeat and surrender

Step Three:
turn and place oneself in alignment

Step Five:
confess and accept our mistakes

Step Seven:
pray and be re-created

Step Nine:
change our current behavior; repair the historical
damage to others

Step Eleven:
improve consciousness to know better;
acquire strength to do better

When I did Step Six with my guide, I was asked to read and highlight the first paragraph on Big Book, page 76, which concerns willingness as the key, and also the Step Six chapter in the Twelve and Twelve.

Our literature specifically suggests *naming* what we identify. In Step Two we name our concept of Power; in Step Four our inventory; in Step Eight our harms; in Step Ten our disturbances. The Big Book does not specifically suggest a Step Six list, but it implies it: "... all the things which we have admitted are objectionable ... take them all" (page 76).

So I made a list. After my prayerful review, I concluded there was nothing that I wanted to retain or continue. I was ready and willing for this removal. The Big Book is quite clear that God, as we understand God, is doing the removing. The implication is that

The lens of our beliefs forms our perceptions:
> Perceptions form our thoughts.
> Thoughts form our feelings.
> Feelings form our attitudes.
> Attitudes form our decisions.
> Decisions form our actions.

Our actions create our life, our karma, our destiny:
> Our internal thermostat is a constellation of beliefs:
> Our beliefs define our normal.
> Our beliefs defend our reality.
> Our beliefs determine our destiny.

We don't see reality as it is; we see reality as we are.
At all times we function to create and maintain our comfort.
We are a constellation of habits: what we practice,
> we become.

we are as powerless over reducing or removing our character disorders as we are over alcohol. We have no effective power to change or even to be willing to be changed. So, in Step Six, we pray: "We ask God to help us be willing."

Step Seven

I reviewed my Step Six reflections and list with my Step guide. He then asked me to read the second paragraph on Big Book, page 76, to read the Step Seven chapter from the Twelve and Twelve, and to create my own Step Seven prayer—not to improve it, but to understand it.

Isn't it wonderful that Step Seven begins with the word *humbly*? What other attitude could we have in light of the suffering our disorders have caused ourselves and others? What other perspective could we have in light of our history of chronic failures to do better, even when we knew better? The Twelve and Twelve's Step Seven chapter is an excellent commentary on humility. The Latin root is *humas*—earth, common, not unique, one of many.

It's equally impressive that the Step Seven prayer begins with "My Creator . . ." (Big Book, page 76). I am broken, inherently flawed. I need to be fixed. I need to be healed. Indeed, I need to be re-created.

I prayed that prayer and also my own Step Seven prayer. Nothing happened. I was painfully aware that I still had the major defect of character that was eroding my professional life, destroying my personal life, and eventually would undermine my program (Big Book, page 70).

That week, in my home group meeting, a man shared that he had prayed specifically for a defect to be removed and had found it freeing. Although that instruction is not in the Big Book, nor in the Twelve and Twelve, I decided to try it based on his experience.

When I got on my knees (to get my *own* attention—not God's), I was about to pray the prayer specifically. But I stopped. I realized I was actually *not willing!* I was attached to the behavior associated with this defect. I was stunned at my unwillingness, but remembered that Step Six suggests prayer for willingness.

I prayed to be willing (to be willing to be willing!). Then I called my Step guide. He congratulated me on my insight, experience, and prayer for willingness. Then he suggested that "willingness without action was fantasy." He suggested that I call him every day to report in and hold myself accountable for my specific behavior. He confirmed that I am powerless over my defect. That's why I pray. But I am responsible for my behavior driven by that defect. That is why I hold myself accountable.

Powerless, so I pray; human, so I call.

Within two days, the behavior connected to this defect ceased, and over time the defect itself diminished and eventually disappeared. This anticipates the formula described in Step Ten: pray; talk; amend; help.

This in turn confirms the final suggestion in the sex inventory: to turn our thoughts to helping others. Both prayer and service are the prescriptions for resolving our spiritual malady. We make a decision to *turn* in Step Three and then, as the result of completing Steps Four through Nine, we discover we have *been turned*. This is the transformation of being awakened, both to a relationship with Other, and also in our relationships with others. Steps Eleven and Twelve are the antidote: self-centeredness becoming Other-centeredness, through Other-centeredness.

. . .

Personal Commitment to Action

Make a commitment.

- *Enter Steps Five, Six, and Seven through the gateway of the Set Aside prayer.*
- *Read and reflect on the referred-to section of the Big Book (pages 72–76) and the Twelve and Twelve (the chapters on Steps Five, Six, and Seven).*
- *Complete the meditations and the suggested work for Steps Five, Six, and Seven.*
- *Meditate daily for guidance with respect to identifying and removing the specific sources of our suffering and disturbance.*
- *Pray specifically for the removal of these defects and the development of our ability to behave in alignment with the desired principles.*

Hold yourself accountable.

- *Have a specific discussion with your sponsor or accountability partner with respect to frequency and format of "telling-on-yourself."*

. . .

We have addressed establishing our relationship with a Power other than our self: Steps One through Three. We have completed our rehabilitation of our relationship with our true self: Steps Four through Seven. Now let's turn to the repair of damages done to others by proceeding to Steps Eight and Nine.

6

We Continue Awakening by Repairing Damage to Others

STEPS EIGHT AND NINE

Step Eight	*Made a list of all persons we had harmed, and became willing to make amends to them all.*
Step Nine	*Made direct amends to such people wherever possible, except when to do so would injure them or others.*

To prepare for this chapter

To prepare, pray the following Set Aside prayer:

Please, _____ [you choose your unique aspect of the Reality you need for this particular phase of this transformative work], *allow me to see the truth of the harmful impact of my self-will on others; grant me the willingness both to change and to effectively repair the damage.*

Keep these questions in mind

- What is the role of prayer and meditation in receiving guidance and power to make amends?

- What is the method of constructing a comprehensive and rigorously honest list of the damage we have caused by our self-centered way of life?

continued

- How do we determine each specific behavior, the circumstances, the actual harm done, and the suggested proportionate and appropriate reparation?

- For each action taken, what and how important is the role of receiving guidance from experienced people and accountability from someone?

- What are the components of forgiveness—releasing and being released?

- What is the role of prayer and meditation in this forgiveness process?

. . .

"Now we go out to our fellows and repair the damage done in the past . . . accumulated out of our effort to live on self-will."

— BIG BOOK, page 76

THE FINAL PHASE OF clearing our channel, as committed to in Step Three, is to make amends: to identify what needs to be changed in ourself and to repair the negative impact of our behavior on others and the world we have inhabited.

Amend means to change. In this process it has two connotations: my *rehabilitation* and the other's *restoration*.

- I am willing (or at least, willing to become willing) to change and to be changed so that I don't continue to create chaos in the world around me.

- I am willing (or at least, willing to become willing) to clean up the negative impact of my destructive behavior.

When reviewing the instructions from the Big Book, pages 76–83, we pay particular attention to the emphasis on the value proposition offered:

> "Remember it was agreed at the beginning *we would go to any lengths for victory over alcohol*" (page 76).

> "Reminding ourselves that we have decided to go to any lengths to find a spiritual experience" (page 79).

We may ask ourselves: When did we decide and agree "to go to any lengths," and how do we know when we're ready?

We return to the introduction to Step Three for the answers: If you "have decided you want what we have and are willing to go to any length to get it—then you are ready to take certain steps" (Big Book, page 58).

We remember that we admitted our powerlessness over alcohol (all our addictions)—in the first half of Step One. We remind ourselves of the unmanageability of our lives (our spiritual malady; the bedevilments) represented by the second half of Step One. Finding a spiritual experience is the antidote to unmanageability, which, in the final analysis, is the antidote to our addiction.

Of course, in the beginning of this amends process we are dealing with our own addiction and "trying to put our lives in order." But, we are told, this will become a secondary motive: "Our real purpose is to fit ourselves to be of maximum service to God and the people about us" (page 77).

How to Change

1. Identify what needs to be changed. What are the specific behaviors?
2. Describe why it needs to be changed. What are the consequences of not changing? Of changing? What is the benefit, the value to me, of changing?
3. List specific action steps it will take to create the desired change.
4. Create a vision of what the change would look and feel like. What are the behaviors resulting from these changes?
5. Keep the vision in mind. Share it with someone. Hold yourself accountable to someone for moving toward this vision.
6. Celebrate success. Accept every small progress as success.

Step Eight

We proceed, in the spirit of Set Aside, to make a list of people and institutions we have harmed by our actions. When I give Step Eight instructions, I do it one component at a time: an incremental unfolding of this most difficult process of naming and accepting the *truth* of the impact of our actions on those around us. Human survival instincts and ego defense mechanisms are built to minimize and resist rigorous honesty. I suggest that sponsees focus only on making a list of names of persons or institutions. I suggest they do not yet focus on the harms and certainly not on the probable amends. I encourage them to stay in prayer, asking for the gift of a complete list.

In prayer we ask for a "quiet and objective" review, for guidance to make a complete list:

- a spontaneous dump from our memory, reviewing our personal history, our relationships, our feelings, our behavior
- a careful review of our chronology in brackets of time or phases of our life
- a review of our Step Four inventory and Step Five experience, when we were encouraged to identify the impact of our dysfunctional attitudes and actions on the people and the world around us

We receive each name as a gift of our prayer and our willingness to be thorough. The Big Book and the Twelve and Twelve suggest we name the results of the following:

- "an accurate and unsparing survey"
- "a deep and honest search of our motives and actions"
- "an accurate and exhaustive survey of our past life"

- "the flaws in our makeup"
- "the personality traits which disturb and injure others"

I suggest that when preparing to make this list some dictionary work may mitigate our resistance and broaden our scope and perspective. I encourage the person to look up and write out definitions for

- hurt
- harm
- wrongs
- betrayal
- diminish
- stress
- infidelity
- disturb
- dishonesty
- manipulation

Once the person has a reasonably complete list of names, I suggest they transfer them to a three-by-five card: one card for each person or institution they think they've harmed. Then they add to the name on the card the action(s) that created the harm(s), along with a sentence about what they thought, felt, or did. Then they identify the specific harm done. The point of Step Eight is: *What is the negative impact of my behavior on others?* We look at it from the recipient's point of view, trying to be specific and complete.

This is not about what we did, how we thought, how we felt— my resentment, my discomfort, my guilt, or my shame. It is *not* about us! It is about them: *How did we diminish the quality of their lives?* Our attitude is to be helpful and forgiving.

The next step is to write out the specific action to repair this damage. Will it be direct—meeting with the person; or emailing, writing, or calling? Will it be indirect? Are there reasons that the amends should not be made, at least not at this time? What are the alternatives so that the sponsee can finish *all* amends? This is where knowledgeable and experienced guidance from a sponsor or Step guide is crucial. And in some cases it is useful to talk to a professional therapist, attorney, accountant, insurance expert, or other professional.

What are the appropriate amends? What is the healthy and effective approach? Are there other people involved in the harmful event? What other people might be considered in the approach to any action? We may want to also indicate on the card: Am I really willing? Somewhat willing? Not willing at all? This list becomes the road map. It becomes a source of accountability: What's next? When am I balking? When am I finished?

Once the Step Eight list or cards have been completed, it is imperative to review each situation with another person, usually one's sponsor or Step guide. Making amends is sacred work. It brings healing, emotional and spiritual, to both parties. It needs to be prepared for by rigorous honesty, a spirit of humility, and a compassionate attitude. It requires guidance from a knowledgeable person with specific experience with each of the actual situations.

The man who guided me is such a person. Even so, he admitted he did not have specific experience with some particular amends I needed to make to a woman. He suggested I contact an experienced woman in the Fellowship and ask her how she would want the situation handled if she had been my victim. I did. She gave me specific instructions based on her experience and also her wisdom from a woman's perspective. (More on this in the next section on Step Nine.)

The point is, I was thoroughly prepared!

Step Nine

"The spiritual life is not a theory. We have to live it," says the Big Book (page 83). Now it's time to make amends.

The word *amends* has two implications: *change* and *repair.*

Change means making a commitment to a consistent effort for different behavior. Again, this is a willingness that includes the assumption of Grace. I am willing to change, and I realize I am powerless to do it. At the same time I am responsible to do it. So I pray: "Please, Holy Spirit, make me whole!" (Use your own term: Higher Power, God, or other, of course.) And I begin to pause before I act—and I experience a *response* rather than a reaction. I continue my effort at "acts contrary to my will." I hold myself accountable to someone for continued specific effort and progress.

We pray and meditate, asking "that we be given strength and direction to do the right thing, no matter what the personal consequences may be" (Big Book, page 79).

The Big Book assumes that we continue to be powerless to objectively assess the truth; we are powerless to actually be really willing to see it clearly and respond fully; we are powerless to accurately evaluate what in us needs to change and what in them calls for our reparation; and we are powerless to really take full responsibility for the truth—reality as it really is. But nevertheless, "We vigorously commenced this way of living as we cleaned up the past" (page 84).

Repair means making a commitment to correct the wrongs done to others, to repair the damage, to make reparation, to bring healing to those we hurt. This is very sacred work. It requires courage and humility, "tact and common sense," "a helpful and forgiving spirit." The Big Book suggests we pray for willingness: "We ask until . . . willingness . . . comes" and "that we be given strength and direction to do the right thing" (page 79). "Before taking drastic action . . . we . . . asked God to help," says the Big Book, and "he had to place the outcome in God's hands " (page 80). The Big Book also suggests meditation as a tool to approach Step Nine: "So we clean house . . . asking each morning in meditation that our Creator show us the way of patience, tolerance, kindliness and love" (page 83). This Step also requires knowledgeable and experienced guidance from others: "Before taking drastic action which might implicate other people we secure their consent. If we have obtained permission, have *consulted with others,* asked God to help and the drastic step is indicated we must not shrink " (page 80; italics added).

It was suggested to me that the most effective approach to and process for making the amends could be summarized as follows:

1. Tell the person the harm done to them, as I see and remember it.

2. Ask the person if they would like to describe any other harm that I haven't mentioned that they experienced and the impact my behavior had on them. Pause and listen to their response. We do not explain or defend ourself.

3. Suggest to the person the actions I propose to take to repair the damage.

4. Ask the person if these suggested actions are appropriate and if there is anything else they would like from me to correct the situation. Pause and listen to their response.

The key points are transparency and willingness to take responsibility for both harm and reparation, and openness to listening and hearing from them their hurt and their suggestion for healing.

My experience is that I have been able to finish my amends each time I have been moved by the God of my understanding (what I call "the Spirit") to engage a Step guide and embark on this Step journey. I needed prayer and guidance from the Spirit; I needed coaching and accountability from the guide. Some amends were direct, some indirect. Some amends called for me to talk to or write the person offended. Some amends called for me to not contact the injured person. Some amends required a creative spiritual approach:

- To dead people: amends can be made graveside, or symbolically in any cemetery.

- To living people who I can't or shouldn't connect with: I can do a specific proportional prayer practice for their healing.

We now ask ourselves: Have I completed my amends?

Earlier, I described seeking counsel from an experienced woman with regard to a harm I had done to a woman in my past. I followed her counsel, made contact with the person, and followed the specific directions. At the end of the call, the woman to whom I was making amends thanked me for the call to acknowledge the past, commenting that "this has been so healing." I had not used those words, but she had had that experience.

The Big Book suggests that when we have made substantial progress ("half way") in completing amends we will begin to experience the promises of freedom. A friend of mine, Dan Sherman, in his *Big Book Awakening* workbook, created a side-by-side contrast of the bedevilments and the promises, suggesting the former are replaced by the latter.[6]

The Bedevilments (Big Book, page 52)		The Promises (Big Book, pages 83–84)
We were having trouble with personal relationships.	→	We will lose interest in selfish things and gain interest in our fellows. Self-seeking will slip away.
We couldn't control our emotional natures.	→	We will comprehend the word *serenity* and we will know peace.
We couldn't make a living.	→	Our whole attitude and outlook upon life will change.
We had a feeling of uselessness.	→	That feeling of uselessness and self pity will disappear.
We were full of fear.	→	Fear of people and of economic insecurity will leave us. We will intuitively know how to handle situations that used to baffle us.
We were unhappy.	→	We are going to know a new freedom and a new happiness.
We couldn't seem to be of real help to other people.	→	No matter how far down the scale we have gone, we will see how our experience can benefit others. We will not regret the past nor wish to shut the door on it.

And, most of all: "We will suddenly realize that God is doing for us what we could not do for ourselves" (page 84).

Forgiveness

Steps Four through Nine represent a process for the "deflation of ego at depth." The diligent application of these Steps removes from us all the obstacles to our relationships with:

- a Power deep down inside
- our true self
- others in our community

The word *forgiveness* surfaces often throughout the Big Book instructions and the Twelve and Twelve commentary. The Twelve Step methodology provides us the same experience of the process of forgiveness described by clinical psychologist Dr. Fred Luskin, in his popular book *Forgive for Good*, an adaptation of his doctoral research thesis on the subject.[7]

1. Name who did it.
2. Understand what happened.
3. Identify my beliefs, my motives; discern "unenforceable rules"; hear my "shoulds."
4. Acknowledge reality as objective and immutable; see the truth about the person(s) and/or circumstances.
5. Accept responsibility for my attitude, expectations, needs, hopes, and especially my dysfunctional actions. I am not responsible for "outside stuff" and need to not take it personally. I am responsible for "inside stuff" and I need to take it personally.
6. Make a decision:
   - to change my story about the person, event, or circumstances.
   - to take action that demonstrates my decision to release them and to be released.

When I looked up the word *forgiveness* in a dictionary, I found reference to letting go of negative emotions and to legally absolving and giving up all claims, which reflects the idea of making "a decision to release them." I was struck by the parallels to Dr. Luskin's forgiveness process and my own experience with my spiritual awakening as the result of the application of the Twelve Step process.

———————— Forgiveness and Freedom ————————

Freedom requires forgiveness:
> Forgiveness is our release of others;
> Forgiveness is our release of ourselves.

Forgiveness in turn requires repentance:
> Repentance happens by naming of our character defects through inventory and the changing of our behavior through amends.

Repentance requires power because we're powerless:
> Powerless to see,
> Powerless to change.

Access to power requires prayer;
Prayer is a decision:
> to believe in,
> to surrender to,
> and to live in,
> The presence of our Higher Power.

In that Presence let us live this day!

————————————————————————————————

I once served on a panel discussion with Dr. Luskin. Talking with him afterward, I observed that the forgiveness process in psychology and in Twelve Step spirituality is the same dynamic, but the words and instructions are different.

Dr. Luskin agreed, and added, "You spiritual people, you Twelve Steppers, have a real advantage."

"What's that?" I asked.

He replied, "You've got God!"

At the same time, twenty years ago, another formulation of forgiveness occurred to me, one that I still find useful:

> *A forgiving person has no past.*
> *An unforgiving person has no future!*

To forgive is not to forget or to change the past. It *did* happen. What happened may have been wrong; it may seem truly unforgiveable and perhaps unforgettable. But to forgive is to release my feelings about these events. I am not responsible for my history; I am responsible for today's feelings about it. I can be free of these events today. With courage I can embrace my decision to release the feelings.

Thus, today, I have hope—the seedbed of my healing.

When we submit to the program of recovery, the Twelve Steps of Alcoholics Anonymous:

- We heal the past.
- We begin to trust in the future.
- We learn to live in the present moment.
- We experience "happy, joyous, and free."

––––––––– Forgiveness Meditation –––––––––

Breathe—in and out—experience my soft belly.

Breathe—in and out—open my heart to the healing Spirit.

Breathe—in and out—remember the hurts of my history.

Remember the ways I have hurt others, how I have been
insensitive to their feelings, betrayed their trust,
disappointed them, caused them suffering.

Be willing to feel regret—to have remorse—to make a
commitment to change my behavior.

Remember the ways I have harmed myself, been unfaithful
to the real me—what I wanted and didn't want for my
life—how I betrayed my inner voice.

Be willing to feel sorrow—to weep for the losses—to
resolve to embrace personal integrity.

Remember the ways I have been wounded by others; these
events *did* happen; I was hurt.

Be willing to feel anguish—to respond with compassion
for others' personal pain—to open our heart to their
history that brought them to such hurtful actions.

Be willing to decide to release my feelings about them and
these events—to let the past be the past and vow to
live the present in loving-kindness.

Grieve my history of hurting and being hurt.

Feel the truth of the pain.

Mourn my history of losses.

Touch the pain to honor it; it is my personal journey of
helplessness and hopelessness.

Feel my breath, feel my pain, feel my tears—be present
and aware of my vulnerability.

Gently breathe and feel the sorrow; embrace it with
tenderness and compassion.

continued

Trust my breath, trust my feelings, trust this process, trust my life.

Resolve to let go of my entire history and to be vulnerable to my present.

Resolve to remember so that I don't repeat.

Resolve to accept reality as it is.

Resolve to hold an open heart to hear the invitation to be present to my self.

Resolve to hold an attitude of compassion for others. All of us are imperfect humans, awkwardly doing the best we can.

Hold the intention of harmony to replace hurt with healing.

Hold the intention of a bridge of tenderness to the separated.

Hold the intention of tender love for the healing and transformation of all.

—————————————————————————————————

. . .

Personal Commitment to Action

Make a commitment.

- *Review my personal history of relationships and identify any damage not addressed.*
- *Create a specific plan to clean up any outstanding debris.*
- *In prayer, and with guidance obtained in my meditation practice, complete the suggested action.*

Hold yourself accountable.

- *Review this assessment and action plan with someone with knowledge and experience for clarification and confirmation.*

. . .

Let us now enter the world of Spirit: our way of living—Steps Ten, Eleven, and Twelve.

7

We Continue Awakening by Dealing with Internal Disturbances

STEP TEN

Step Ten	*Continued to take personal inventory and when we were wrong promptly admitted it.*

To prepare for this chapter

In preparation for this chapter, please pray a version of your Set Aside commitment to be taken to a new place of consciousness.

Keep these questions in mind

- Am I aware of my tendency to fall asleep, unintentionally unconscious?
- Am I committed to a daily practice to stay awake, intentionally conscious?
- Am I willing to work at keeping my channel clear to enable
  - a vital prayer and meditation practice?
  - a life of compassionate service based on universal principles?
- Am I willing to have a guide or teacher?
- Am I willing to be accountable for my daily inventory practice and my daily behavior?

STEP TEN IS A TOOL that captures and releases the transformative power of Steps One through Nine for the continued "deflation of ego at depth." The fact is, we never transcend our basic humanity: we are finite body, mind, and will: all functions that regularly misfire. Step Ten is the tool that keeps open the gate to the world of Spirit, the instrument through which we establish and foster emotional sobriety.

The Twelve and Twelve (page 90) suggests a spiritual axiom: "Whenever I'm disturbed there is something wrong with me." It further explains that Step Ten is a "spot-check" inventory. That is, on the spot, at the very moment of our "disturbance," we pause, taking responsibility for that disturbance. We apply the Step Ten formula immediately—not in writing, not at night. We are to address the disturbance right now as a method of dealing with this very moment's disturbance.

Our body's survival instinct is to react, generating emotions. These feelings direct our attention and behavior toward what we feel, at that time, is in our best interest. Our mind's function is to receive all this data, to think, perceive, and know (intuit) what's truly best for us in that moment.

The mind's problem is that it is a lens formed by our biology, psychology, social framework, and experiences. It sees reality as *we* are, not as reality objectively *is*. Our will—that function in us that makes us uniquely human—relies on our instincts, our feelings, and our intuitions to make its choice for action. If any of these prior functions go awry, we will make unhealthy choices and therefore take unhealthy actions.

Step Ten is our spiritual instrument of intervention, for re-calibration of our various systems for surviving and flourishing.

How Step Ten Works

The promises articulated on pages 83 and 84 of the Big Book "will always materialize *if we work for them*" (italics added). The initial work is Step Ten. The continued work is to *improve and enlarge* our consciousness through our practice of Steps Eleven and Twelve, respectively. The work of these three steps Bill W. calls "our way of living."

We have walked the path of the "destruction of self-centeredness": Steps One through Nine. As we're cleaning up the past, doing Step Nine, we are to grow "in understanding" (through meditation and prayer) "and effectiveness" (through consistent practice of principles). Now we have turned, have been turned, " . . . in all things to the Father of Light who presides over us all" (Big Book, page 14). We have emerged from the world of self, and we have entered the world of Spirit.

And we can continue to address these disturbances "when they crop up" (page 84). *When*, not *if!* So we continue to watch for selfishness, dishonesty, resentment, and fear.

These are the major components of the original problems examined in the Step Four inventory. So we apply the remedy, the solution we applied in Steps Five through Nine:

1. "We ask God *at once* to remove them": Prayer . . . because we have experienced that we are powerless—Steps Six/Seven: "My Creator . . . ."

2. "We discuss them with someone *immediately*": Confession . . . because we're human and want to hold ourselves accountable—Step Five: No secrets.

3. "Make amends quickly . . .": Love and tolerance becomes our code . . . because our intention is to be a healthy human being living in harmony in a community of human beings—Steps Eight/Nine: Forgiveness.

4. "We *resolutely* turn our thoughts to someone we can help" . . . because the ultimate remedy for our self-centeredness is the "turning" to be other-centered—Step Twelve: Service.

The Twelve and Twelve describes this formula as the Step Ten inventory process to be used on the spot:

- to take "a continuous look at our assets and liabilities"
- "to keep in emotional balance"
- "to learn and grow"
- to create "a habit of self-searching, accurate self-appraisal, unsparing self-survey"
- to admit and accept the truth
- to correct what is wrong, to rebalance those excesses of negative emotions
- to live serenely

We have *recovered*, as the Big Book suggests (pages 84–85). We have been placed in a position of neutrality with respect to our addiction. We are not fighting. Sanity—healthy thinking—has returned. We are living within a spiritual shield—protected, invulnerable to the onslaught of our addiction obsession (imagine the force fields in *Star Wars*). We recoil from temptation as we would from a hot flame. This is in direct contrast to being in the grip of our addiction, repeatedly putting our hand on a hot stove, not remembering that last time it burned us (page 24). We have a new attitude: "We are safe and protected." We have received the gift of *physical* sobriety.

But we are *not cured.*

We need to "keep in fit spiritual condition" (page 85). We cannot rest on our laurels or past accomplishments, which is yesterday's spiritual work. We have a daily reprieve, a stay of execution. Each day has its own work.

Psychiatrist Dr. Harry Tiebout confirmed in his pioneering work on alcoholism in the 1950s that Bill W. got it right: the first nine Steps deflate the ego at depth. But the ego has an uncanny way of regenerating itself.

Remember the "dimmer switch" discussed earlier: it is spring-loaded to go backward. We need to lean gently into it, pushing it forward: one notch at a time, one day at a time, one spiritual practice at a time.

How do we grow in both *understanding* and *effectiveness?* The Big Book connects Steps Ten and Eleven with this transition. "Every day is a day when we must carry the vision of God's will into all of our activities" (page 84). Whose vision? My vision . . . of God's will. The purpose of meditation is guidance, the "knowledge of God's will for us" part of Step Eleven. Each morning we sit to envision our day, receiving both knowledge and power.

We ask in prayer: "How can I best serve Thee—Thy will (not mine) be done" (page 85). In meditation, we are using our mind to reflect on and receive guidance about this invitation from our Higher Power today. We ask (pray) about our daily activities: *"Think* about the twenty-four hours ahead" (in meditation).

We ask (pray) about operating principles: Who am I going to be today? "We *consider* our plans for the day" and "employ our mental faculties with assurance" (page 86). This is the proper use of our mind in meditation.

The next suggestion for maintaining our spiritual condition is to "exercise our willpower" along this line all we wish. We decide, with our free will, to seek the truth—the immutable guiding principles of reality; and to align our decisions and actions with these perceived truths—to be in harmony with reality as we see it, to the best of our ability. This is the proper use of the will (page 85).

The body depends on instinct; the mind develops a reliance on intuition. With continued practice, our will learns to receive, trust, and respond to inspiration (*spiros*—the breath of God in us).

Emotional Sobriety through Step Ten

Through Step Ten we are attempting to keep our channel clear of obstacles to our relationship with Power, with ourself, and with others. On the spot we identify disturbances and take the indicated necessary actions to eliminate them.

———————— Finding Our Center of Gravity ————————

The solution to being disturbed is not to identify the solution to the perceived problem, but to identify the reason within myself for being disturbed. The problem can't really be controlled or managed outside myself. When the source of being disturbed is within, and the observer of being disturbed is also within—then I have an object and subject that is under my influence and can be managed. I realize the perceived problem is but the symptom of the problem. The real problem is my reaction to it.

When I assume the witness role, observing the source of my disturbance as internal, as my perception of the problem, I begin to grind the lens of my beliefs to better show reality *as it is,* not distorted to perceive myself as the victim of outside forces. If we are centered, we are not as influenced by those forces.

Thus my goal is to have my center of gravity within me, rather than outside me.

——

We have received the gift of physical sobriety and are now finding emotional sobriety. We are using the faculties of our neocortex to manage both our mind and our will: the emotional feelings produced by the limbic system and also the biological drives flowing from the brain stem system. We have a thermostat. Thus, we are now organically inclined to self-regulation and work for conscious management and containment to produce:

- sustained abstinence
- sanity; healthy thinking
- personal responsibility
- harmony
- equilibrium
- acceptance
- serenity
- joy and happiness
- healing and wholeness
- freedom
- accountability

- integrity and authenticity
- understanding
- effectiveness
- resilience; openness to change
- right relationships
- interdependence
- self-actualization
- living the middle way
- realization of our true self

With as much consciousness as we can muster and sustain, we manage our thoughts, feelings, and instincts; we pause before taking any action. We cut the internal and external puppet strings and take responsibility for all our thoughts, all our feelings, and, especially, all our actions, as well as their impact on others. We identify, establish, and hold on to our true self. We keep our center of gravity within ourself. We consciously decide what we want or don't want to do. We stop living our *story* and start living our life.

"We have begun to sense the flow of . . . Spirit into us. To some extent we have become God-conscious. We have begun to develop this vital sixth sense" (Big Book, page 85). We have an effective GPS: God positioning system!

––––––––––– Being and Becoming ––––––––––––

> Being is eternal;
>
> Becoming is temporal.
>
> What we love is what we become.
>
> I resolve not to live in collusion with my delusions.
>
> I resolve to live as a Loving being.

––

We pause and *pray,* on the spot: "Not my will, but Thine be done."

We pause and *meditate,* on the spot: Visualize how we might have done better.

We ask: Am I doing to others as I would have them do to me?

The formula for change is captured in the Twelve and Twelve (page 95). On a daily basis:

- We spot (we identify).
- We admit.
- We correct.

This technique provides us an opportunity to restart our day at any time. It allows a Power greater than self to continue to shape us. This is the essence of character-building and good living.

Inventory Meditation at Night

The Twelve and Twelve's Step Ten chapter suggests an evening inventory where we "draw a balance sheet," noting

- our honest regret for harms done.
- our genuine gratitude for blessings received.
- our willingness to try for better things.

The Big Book is clear: Step Ten is used during the day as an intervention and correction to our cycle of disturbances—on the spot.

The Twelve and Twelve makes clear that inventory and meditation go hand-in-glove. Inventory removes the clouds that block the Sunlight of the Spirit in us, to us, and then through us to others. We are built to be a channel of Light. In Step Ten, we remove the obstacles in our channel. In Step Eleven, we fill our channel with Light. In Step Twelve, we work to have the Light in us seep out to our community. Step Ten is the inventory we do *on the spot* during our waking moments during our working day.

The Big Book's Step Eleven discussion contains suggestions for inventory "when we retire at night"—perhaps acknowledging that during the day we are not always awake to being disturbed. Actually, we are asleep dreaming that we are awake. Or we are so disturbed that we are in a "white out"—incapable of any self-reflection, held hostage by our emotions of the day.

When we take a little time in the evening, after the day's hustle-bustle has quieted down, especially within ourselves, we are able to discern unhealthy moments during the day. These become grist for the mill of the next morning's meditation, listening for guidance and then planning for the day: What will I *do,* and who am I invited to *be* today?

Step Ten is the spiritual technology that provides emotional sobriety; this in turn enables us to *improve* and *enlarge* our spiritual sobriety: Steps Eleven and Twelve, respectively.

Step Twelve's importance is obvious. The bulk of the Big Book addresses Step Twelve and how the Twelve Step process manifests:

living our life based on spiritual, universal principles; carrying the message of the promise of an awakening.

There is the hope of freedom both from our addiction and also from our anxiety. The problems of both halves of Step One have been addressed. In other words, we are promised the power to live an integrated and authentic personal life that gives us: purpose, meaning, context, and value.

This is a very hope-filled "Vision for Me."

. . .

Personal Commitment to Action

1. Make a commitment.

   I will include in my morning meditation resolutions:
   - *to be diligent about watching for my internal disturbances during the day—to live conscious and mindful.*
   - *to implement the pause and use the Step Ten formula to foster my intentional consciousness.*

2. Hold yourself accountable.

   I will :
   - *have one or more Step Ten partners who have agreed to collaborate as needed in my daily practice of personal truth and transparency.*
   - *include in my nightly review meditation an accountability to my Higher Power for this practice.*

• • •

8

We Enlarge Our Awakening by Carrying the Message and Practicing the Principles

STEP TWELVE

Step Twelve	*Having had a spiritual awakening as the result of these steps, we tried to carry this message to alcoholics, and to practice these principles in all our affairs.*

To prepare for this chapter

Please pray a version of your Set Aside prayer to be taken to a new experience of commitment and compassion.

Keep these questions in mind

- Do I really believe in my free will, my personal responsibility, and the value of my awakened consciousness?
- Do I understand and take seriously the Big Book's warning that "we are not cured," that we have "a daily reprieve contingent on the maintenance of our spiritual condition"?
- What exactly does it mean: "the maintenance of our spiritual condition"?
- Am I willing to develop a consistent daily practice of principles and service?
- Do I really believe in enlarging my consciousness by responding to the Spirit's invitation to use my unique gift of service?
- Do I hold as my primary question to be asked and answered: "How can I best serve Thee?" "How can I help?"

"Practical experience shows that nothing will so much insure immunity from drinking as intensive work with other alcoholics."
— BIG BOOK, page 89

EACH AND ALL OF US ARE, at the very least, containers and channels of life and energy. Each and all of us have our own beliefs about this. Our beliefs determine our perceptions, which eventually determine our choices and actions. There are always consequences to a person's actions, positive or negative, desired or undesired. What is the nature of this will, the power of choice?

Higher Self: the best in me = *My* story?

Human Spirit: the best in us = *Our* story?

Universal Spirit (or Holy, Creative, Great Spirit), the Source of all there is = *The* story?

Each person's interpretation is good enough as long as each lives consistently in integrity with it. We all need

- an inventory practice—when disturbed, taking personal responsibility for the consequences of our behavior
- a consciousness practice—a daily practice of improving awareness and making healthier choices
- a compassion practice—an organic orientation, based on principles and altruistic action on behalf of the balance of humanity

The effective use of our willpower to consent to the action of a Power other than our self is the foundation of a spiritual practice. What is the litmus test of an authentic spiritual practice? Perhaps it's found in the practitioner's daily life: Is it a life lived according to spiritual principles and an organic personal commitment to helping, to making a positive contribution to reduce suffering?

The Context for Step Twelve: An Overview

The commentary on Step Eleven in the Big Book ends with the words "Faith without works is dead" (page 88), confirming that belief without action is empty and inauthentic. There is an organic relationship between improving consciousness and having a commensurate energy for connectedness and compassion. In his story in the Big Book, Bill W. comments, "If an alcoholic failed to perfect and enlarge his spiritual life through work and self-sacrifice for others, he could not survive the certain trials and low spots ahead" (pages 14–15). Five chapters of the Big Book focus on Step Twelve, comprising 41 percent of its pages (chapters 7 through 11). Step Twelve itself (page 60) confirms:

- the promise—"Having had a spiritual awakening"
- the process—"as *the* result of these steps" (italics added)
- the invitation—"we tried to carry this message to alcoholics"
- the guidelines— " . . . and to practice these principles in all our affairs"

"We have come to believe 'God' would like us to keep our heads in the clouds with 'God' but that our feet ought to be firmly planted on earth," says the Big Book. This " . . . is where our work must be done . . . a life of sane and happy usefulness" (page 130).

The Content of Step Twelve

The content of Step Twelve has three segments: the promise of a spiritual awakening, a process that includes a precise methodology, and an invitation to carry the message.

The promise: Spiritual awakening

A spiritual experience and a spiritual awakening both lead to a radical change in personality—a shift in the way a person thinks, feels, and behaves. The Big Book's appendix II (pages 567–68) confirms this. But it also notes how they differ: one (spiritual experience) is fast, the other (spiritual awakening) is tediously slow—the difference between a light switch and a dimmer switch. The real key to understanding and appreciating this change is that it is done to us, not by us. Although we do a considerable amount of work—prayer, meditation, reflection, reading, writing, discussion—over an extended period of time, the results are much larger than our contribution to the effort. They are immeasurably disproportionate. I like to say, "I can't get here from there, but here I am!"

The word *spiritual* I view with the most extreme inclusivity. Of course, Bill Wilson's original intent was to reflect the work of Spirit, God, Higher Power. But my experience demonstrates that it can also be seen in the terms psychologist Abraham Maslow used. In his "hierarchy of needs," reaching the level of self-actualization offers a higher human purpose and fulfillment, a sense of meaning and value.

This is consistent with the Buddhist and other Eastern religions' interpretation of "higher self"; the psychologist's terminology of the true self; and the use of words such as Nature, Universe, or Life Force in various non-sectarian spiritual practices.

The product of the Step methodology is to produce the necessary organic transformation of the human individual to manifest the highest level of its very nature, the ideal and authentic self-reality:

- a mind that is fully conscious
- a will that is fully aligned with Reality
- a being that is fully integrated

The process: Precise methodology

The Twelve Steps have a rhythm. It's an alternating rhythm, referring to what we *know* consciously and what we *decide* freely.

All of the even-numbered Steps refer to *knowing* as a prelude to action. They name

- the source of our Power (Step Two)
- the internal obstacles to that Power (Step Four)
- our inclinations and behaviors manifesting these internal obstacles (Step Six)
- the impact of these dysfunctional behaviors on others (Step Eight)
- an awareness of how to address disturbances in our lives and return to equanimity (Step Ten)
- a commitment to foster compassion, enlarging our will's capacity and inclination to help by living a life of right action based on principles (Step Twelve)

All the odd-numbered Steps are invitations to specific actions:

- to accept defeat and surrender (Step One)
- to decide to *turn* and be in alignment (Step Three)
- to become transparent to reduce and eliminate obstacles (Step Five)
- with humility, to accept our fundamental powerlessness to change and ask for help through divine intervention and our own accountability (Step Seven)
- to strive to change the source and therefore the symptoms of our dysfunctions; to create and implement a plan of repair of damage to others through healing and forgiveness (Step Nine)
- to adopt a daily practice of prayer and meditation to *improve* our mind's consciousness and enable right thinking, and therefore right living (Step Eleven)

You can choose to explain this process from a theological vantage point or a more scientific one. The explanation really doesn't matter. The results are the same, and also inevitable. If a person diligently applies this Twelve Step process to their personal development, gets guidance from an experienced person to whom they hold themselves transparently accountable, and completes their Step Eight and Nine amends, they will experience a shift in consciousness. If they subsequently foster this change with a daily practice of the outlined way of life, the experience will not only be sustained, but it will evolve to a broader and deeper awakening. With each click forward, the dimmer switch releases more light. The really good news is this light is infinite.

The invitation: Carry the message

What is the message? Of course there are a variety of experiences, understandings, opinions, and interpretations. As spiritual psychologist Ken Wilber proclaims, "Everybody is correct!" Correct, that is, from their own level of personal development of consciousness.

But let's look at the context. "Having had a spiritual awakening as the result of these steps, we tried to carry this message . . . ." Perhaps the Big Book authors intended what they wrote! We can have a spiritual awakening if we do these Steps—as precisely experienced and documented by the conscience of that initial group of one hundred AAs. That's confirmed on page 45: "Lack of power is our dilemma." Notice: lack of power, *not* alcohol! "We had to find a *Power greater than ourselves!*"

The message is the miracle. *We can't get here from there—but here we are!*

It does not matter what we think, feel, want, expect, or even believe. What does matter—and it's vitally important—is what we *do,* the actions we take.

You may look and dress like a traveler; you may have a travel agent; you may have a traveler's guidebook and ticket; you may be in the train station; you may be reading and talking about traveling. But unless you get and stay on the train, you will not be taken to the intended and promised destination. Please hear the real implications here. When you get on the train—that is, our personal application of each Step—the train takes us to our destination. We start working the Steps, and they begin and continue to work us. As long as we stay gently pressed up against the dimmer switch, the dial moves forward; the light brightens. We collaborate. Our willingness powers Grace; Grace empowers our willingness. We organically co-create our awakening.

The Role of a Sponsor

The word *sponsor* does not appear in the Big Book (through page 164). There were several opportunities to use the word if it had actually been part of the Alcoholics Anonymous culture when the Big Book was written in 1939. The Big Book uses the term "spiritual advisor" for Step Three (page 63) and "suitable person" for Step Five (page 74). On page 18, an entire italicized paragraph describes what might perhaps qualify such a person, and the next full paragraph profiles that person. But no mention of a sponsor. Yet the word *sponsor* is generously sprinkled throughout the Twelve and Twelve, which was published in 1953, just fourteen years later.

The AA General Service Office has a pamphlet on sponsorship based on Alcoholics Anonymous' experience. Many people have written on the topic, including Bill Wilson and Father Ed Dowling in their letters collected in the book *The Soul of Sponsorship*. Hamilton B., in his book *Twelve Step Sponsorship*, offers many ingredients for what makes a good sponsor. One of my favorites is his description of a sponsor as a person who is really enjoying their sobriety.

In my early recovery, I needed a sponsor who could teach me about the basics of the Twelve Step Fellowship, its culture and practices. I found one who was also a very seasoned sounding board for living sober: relationships, family, work, finances, fun, and finding balance in life. He was the first person to whom I held myself fully accountable.

Eventually, I needed to go outside that relationship to get the help I needed with understanding the Big Book, applying each Step, and deeply experiencing the actual program of recovery leading to a spiritual awakening. I called them my Step guides—these people whom I engaged across the years: 1988, 1991, 1994, 2003. They were not sponsors, nor did they become personal friends. They were more like project managers.

Obviously the ideal is a person who resonates both with your current needs and your personal evolution.

My experience shows me that sponsorship is the single most important tool in the recovery toolbox—tools that include meetings, prayer and meditation, the Twelve Steps, the Big Book and Twelve and Twelve, service, sponsorship. All are valuable, but if you have a sponsor, an active relationship with an experienced person, you'll take part in all the rest.

The Problem and Its Solution

The turning that is signaled throughout the Big Book as the solution to the problem is the opposite of the problem. The problem is "Selfishness—self-centeredness" (page 62). What's the solution? Other-centeredness! Step Eleven confirms that this means improving our relationship with Other, the Mystery. Step Twelve confirms that this means *enlarging* our spiritual life "through work and self-sacrifice for others" (page 14).

These two Steps are like a coin—fully integrated, flip sides of the same Reality.

Working, *living*, Step Twelve is an organic development. Usually we start with "acts contrary to our will." Eventually, there is a deep natural energy in us that brings us to help others in our own unique way, because we really want to.

This turning to help others is in fact the inoculation we need to provide immunity to the onslaught of the obsession and delusion—"Nothing will so much insure immunity from drinking (addiction/brokenness) as intensive work with other alcoholics," says the Big Book on page 89. Or helping any other human being, in my experience.

We have a physical and mental deficiency and also a spiritual malady, encompassing both halves of Step One (see page 64). The solution to the source and manifestations of this cancer is our turning to Other—a Power greater than ourselves—for help for ourselves and our turning to *others* to bring help to them. As we discussed earlier, this is the basic recommended solution in Step Four: to find freedom from deep resentment, to experience relief from our fears, and to receive guidance with our sexual behavior. This is especially visible in the recap formula for staying awake as outlined in Step Ten: Pray, talk, amend, help!

We decide to turn to Other and others. We experience that we are *turned*.

Before we are turned, we are like the Dead Sea, so called because no life grows in it. It is stagnant because it has no outlet. After we are turned, we are like the Sea of Galilee, which is vibrant with plant and fish life; it has many outgoing rivulets and streams allowing the water to flow and remain fresh and life-sustaining.

Each of us has a unique history. There has never been anybody exactly like me or you: biology, psychology, sociology, personal experiences. Each of us is as unique as our fingerprint: there never was, is not now, and never will be a fingerprint like ours. So each of us has special gifts as the result of our uniqueness. Thus, perhaps we can help someone who cannot be helped by anyone else. If we don't use our gift, it will never appear in the world again.[8]

This is our invitation—to find our gift, to foster our gift, and to use our gift to leave this world a slightly better place for our being in it.

Each of us is or can be a lantern that stands by the path lighting the way for others. The light I shine is my experience, so that others can walk securely in this light and have their own experience. I am not the Light; I am the channel of the Light so others can be en*light*ened.

In a saying often attributed to St. Francis but of unknown origin, we are wisely counseled, "Preach the Good News wherever you are; if you have to, use words." Similarly, another saying often attributed to Gandhi suggests that we "Be the change you want to see in the world." In the same spirit, Winston Churchill is reputed to have said, "We make a living by what we get; we make a life through what we give."

Our own Twelve Step culture contains many of these same paradoxical wisdom sayings:

- When we concede powerlessness, we access power.
- When we release and forgive, we are released and forgiven.
- When we give it away, we keep it.
- We receive to the extent we give.
- When we help others, our life flourishes.
- The more I help others, the better I feel.
- The more I bring happiness to others, the happier I am.
- When I do better, I eventually know and feel better.
- The more committed I am to my spirituality, the more truly human I become.

The Practice: Using Universal Principles in All Our Affairs

Webster defines *principle* as "a basic truth or proposition that serves as the foundation for a system of belief, behavior, or a chain of reasoning, a source of an objective reality; a general law of nature that controls how something works or explains why something happens."

The Big Book uses the word *principles* as a synonym for the Steps themselves. Apparently, the author did not want to use the same word in consecutive sentences. We're not told specifically what the principle is for each Step, nor are we given a list of principles. But in chapter 7 we learn how to carry the message. It seems reasonable to see the balance of the Big Book as applications of the guidance to "practice these principles in all your affairs." Chapter 8, "To Wives," guides us on principles in our significant relationships; chapter 9, "The Family Afterward," tells about applying the principles in our family life; chapter 10, "To Employers," shows how to use principles in our workplace in our workplace. Chapter 11, "A Vision for You," describes practicing principles in our community, especially in our Twelve Step Fellowship.

To fill the gap suggested by the Big Book, several attempts have been made to make a list of principles that Step Twelve challenges us to practice "in all our affairs." Using these shoulders to stand on, I've compiled one too, which you'll find in appendix C. Perhaps this can be a tool for meditation—a litmus test for current behavior or a vision statement for desired future behavior.

These principles are universal, that is, immutable. Some people call them spiritual principles. Perhaps, in the final analysis, they are just objective reality—the way it is, the way life works. We all have our story about the origin of reality. But does the story really matter? Or is it the observable reality that is the truth?

In physics there is the principle (law) of gravity. It does not matter what I think, feel, know, want, expect, or believe about gravity. If I leap off a thirty-story building wanting to fly, no matter how well I have prepared, I am going to fall and probably die. Gravity has no opinion and no preference. It is an immutable law of reality.

Perhaps we can apply the same thinking to the world of human reality of consciousness and action. Humans have consciousness and free will. But there seem to be universal guidelines to ensure the survival of humanity and the probability of individual happiness. These have been institutionalized in civilized practices throughout the centuries. These are the rules or laws recommended and enforced by each society. These are human principles.

But various other sets of guidelines have been accumulated throughout history by and for those individuals who are seeking a deeper consciousness, spiritual development, or enlightenment. These are spiritual principles.

Karma is essentially the word used to describe the absolute predictable outcome of a lifetime of consistent behaviors. There are always consequences to and from our actions. If we live in accordance with certain principles (universal, higher, human, spiritual?), we will experience positive results. If, on the other hand, we live transgressing these immutable principles, we will experience negative results. This is the source of suffering. Life will crush us.

We create our own misery. God doesn't punish us; people don't persecute us; life is not unfair. Reality just is reality—but only 100 percent of the time. But as Victor Frankl observed in his book *Man's Search for Meaning*, "The last of one's freedoms is to choose one's attitude in any given circumstance."[9]

· · ·

Personal Commitment to Action

1. Make a commitment.

   I will include in my morning meditation:
   - *a prayer to be helpful*
   - *a reflection on one principle each day for understanding and inspiration*

2. Hold yourself accountable.

   I will :
   - *call my sponsor regularly and be transparent*
   - *discuss my experience with aligning all my behavior with principles*

· · ·

A Vision for You

"You will find release from care, boredom and worry . . .
Life will mean something."

— BIG BOOK, page 152

Keep these questions in mind

- What exactly is "our way of life"?
- Do I live a consistent practice of . . .
  - spot-checking my internal disturbances? (Step Ten)
  - seeking guidance? (Step Eleven)
  - practicing compassion based on principles? (Step Twelve)
- Do I have a sponsor with whom I hold myself accountable on a regular basis?

THE BIG BOOK CONSISTENTLY refers to Steps Ten, Eleven, and Twelve as "our way of living."

By getting to and through Step Nine's amends, we complete our rite of passage and begin living *emotional* sobriety, taking full responsibility for our thoughts, feelings, and actions (Step Ten). By entering the world of Spirit, we commit to *spiritual* sobriety—acknowledging our humanity through accepting both our powerlessness and our accountability (Steps Eleven and Twelve). Thus, our way of living is

- clearing the channel; being awake to falling asleep (Step Ten)

- filling the channel; improving our consciousness through consistent practice of being in the presence of Consciousness (Step Eleven)
- opening the channel; enlarging our consciousness through living by principles and compassionate service to all those around us, especially those in need of our specific experience (Step Twelve)

Our free will's function is to decide and initiate the selected actions.

Living Our Truth: Our Way of Life

We humans define ourselves by our actions. What makes us unique is both our ability to know and our ability to decide to take action. We indeed are the sentient being that knows that it knows—that has the power of self-reflection, that makes truly free choices and takes truly voluntary actions.

What we see may be an illusion: a false perception of an external reality. What we believe may be a delusion: a false thought or perception about an objective reality. These are misrepresentations of truth—they are always subjective. We may not see that we really don't see; we may not know that we really don't know.

But what we do is what we believe. How we behave represents our truth—it is always objective. What we do is who we are. What we do represents what we believe. How we behave reveals our core values. Our head regularly tells us a lie; our feet always tell the truth.

The litmus test of our emotional and spiritual development is the choices we make and the actions we take. Our behavior reveals our personal character.

Reality is not what we want, think, feel, or need. Reality is what it is—100 percent objective—but only 100 percent of the time.

Our sixth sense is an awareness of the fourth dimension. By submitting to and applying these Twelve Steps, we improve our consciousness. These Twelve Steps are a method that provides the foundation and functioning of our way of living:

- making a commitment to stay awake: Step Ten
- fostering our conscious contact: Step Eleven
- enlarging our consciousness: Step Twelve

We have a practice.

We practice our practice.

We're faithful to our practice.

Our practice is faithful to us.

We might protect ourselves by building four thick walls around us: walls of anger, secrets, fear, and dishonesty. But those walls turn out to be a prison: the bondage of self-centeredness. The bars melt and the walls crumble when we decide to turn to the "Contractor" and co-construct our real self by providing a place of comfort for others.

Spiritual Sobriety

We are now looking at reality through a contemplative lens—one that has been shaped by the story of unity.

Our vision: Head, clouds; feet, ground.

We are reminded that

- God will provide what we need if we keep close to God and perform God's work well (Big Book, page 63).

- "We are in the world to play the role [God] assigns" (page 68).

- Our "job now is to be at the place . . . of maximum helpfulness to others" (page 102).

In a different order, these three parts echo the subtitle in Ken Wilber's book *Integral Meditation: Mindfulness as a Way to Grow Up, Wake Up, and Show Up in Your Life*. We might view it this way: Step Ten: We wake up. Step Eleven: We grow up. Step Twelve: We show up.

This spiritual reality can also be stated as two principles: the internal and external, the thought and the action. For example, Buddhism's two primary principles are Wisdom and Compassion. Judaism's two primary laws are "Love the LORD thy G_d with all thy heart, and with all thy soul, and with all thy strength" (Deuteronomy 6:5) and "You shall love your neighbor as yourself" (Leviticus 19:18). For Christianity, they are stated similarly: "Love the Lord your God with all your heart, and with all your soul and with all your mind" (Matthew 22:37) and "This is my commandment: that you love each other as I have loved you" (John 15:12).

Radio talk-show host Dennis Prager, in his *Happiness Hour* series, declared that anyone who is targeting happiness as their life's goal will never be happy. He suggested that happiness is a by-product, not a product. My happiness is a by-product of my relationship with my Higher Power and my service to people.

Perhaps all these conclusions are so because consciously or intuitively they reflect the reality of who we are as humans: sentient beings with a mind and will, with the unique ability to be conscious and to make voluntary decisions for creative actions.

Full human development is contingent on *improving* our consciousness and *enlarging* our compassion. Our development is a journey, not a destination. In fact, the journey is the destination.

This journey is facilitated when we find a path, a teacher, and a community.

I sincerely hope this book has shone the light on the path of Intentional Consciousness. Many of us may have had the experience that when we begin walking our path consciously, the teacher appears. And thus we are led to our community—a Fellowship of the Spirit.

Thank you for joining me on this journey of awakening our consciousness and enlarging our capacity for compassion.

. . .

Living in the World of Spirit—
Practicing Intentional Consciousness

REALITY IS WHAT IT IS, independent of my perceptions, thoughts, feelings, and desires. But my beliefs *determine* my perceptions, thoughts, feelings, and desires; my reactions and behaviors. They are the lenses through which I see. I do not see the lenses themselves—they are the filters that determine my understanding of reality. I have beliefs about myself, about others, and about how the world works. I see what I know; my reality is a projection of who I am.

These beliefs are unconscious. I do not know that I do not see reality as it is. Until the unconscious is made conscious, I experience my life and the consequences of my behavior as an unfortunate series of acts of fate, or worse, the fault of others. I live unconsciously as a perennial victim.

The journey to adulthood, to emotional and spiritual maturity, is the willingness to seek and accept what is; to let go of old ideas, interpretations, judgments, rejections, denials, and attachments. It is the readiness to challenge the "shoulds" and to identify delusions and unenforceable rules. *It is the willingness to live radically in the Here and Now.*

I offer these final questions to ask yourself as you "trudge the Road of Happy Destiny." You might use them as a source of reflection in your morning practice.

- Am I willing to release the past? Can I? Am I willing to ask for help?

- Am I willing to begin to accept reality as it is, not as I want or expect it to be—past and present? What would that look like?

- Am I willing to take actions contrary to my normal reaction—to act better than I think, feel, or want?

- Am I willing to accept full responsibility for my thoughts, feelings, attitudes, and, especially, my actions?

- Am I willing to examine the motives—the beliefs, thoughts, feelings, values—that drive my behavior?

- Am I willing to be reasonably undefended? To be transparent? Am I willing to evaluate and begin to repair the damage I've inflicted on others?

- Am I willing to release my story and to change my vocabulary about it—to reframe my view about my current life, detaching it from my history?

- Do I accept that I am truly powerless over realities outside of me: events and people? That I am fully responsible for realities inside of me—beliefs, thoughts, feelings, decisions, and the consequences of my behavior?

- Do I trust the human spirit—mine and others'—enough to be vulnerable?

- Do I believe that I co-create my life by rigorously operating on spiritual principles in a community of like-minded pilgrims?

- Am I willing to begin each day by writing down one thing that I am grateful for—a new item each day?

- Am I willing to be healed and made whole, even if I have no idea of what that would look like, or even how to begin the process?

- Am I willing to make a commitment to freedom from negativity, to holding a positive attitude, to submitting to accountability for being restored to my true self?

- Am I willing to ask for help and also offer help? Do I believe that both actions will open my heart?

- Do I believe that Love is the beginning, the middle, and the goal?

- Do I believe everything that happens has but one purpose—to make us aware of our true nature and to remove the impediments to that awareness?

- Do I believe that Love is
  - our Source . . . whence we come?
  - our Sustenance . . . in which we live and breathe and have our being?
  - our Sanctuary . . . toward which we evolve to complete union?

When we are willing to explore these questions and embrace the answers, we are taken to a new consciousness—we have entered the fourth dimension.

Our life's journey is to realize that our thirst for the Infinite cannot be satisfied by what is finite. In the words of Blaise Pascal, "The hole in us is in the shape of God."

Welcome to the world of the Spirit.

. . .

Acknowledgments

I thank my companion, Allen Berger, Ph.D., for the caring and effective therapy that brought insight and stability to my early recovery from alcoholism. His openness and sense of adventure allowed us to develop a personal friendship as we explored a broader spiritual awakening through Richard Rohr's Men's Rite of Passage and the introduction to the world of the contemplative. Cooperating with the invitation of the "wee small voice," we became partners in bringing our combined psychological and spiritual knowledge and experience to others in workshops and retreats about the new frontier: emotional sobriety. Finally, he referred Hazelden Publishing to me when asked about a possible author for this very book on Step Eleven.

Thanks to my editor, Sid Farrar, for his coaching and cheerleading; his attitude and encouragement have been truly energizing and inspirational. His thoughtful insights and suggestions have improved the effectiveness of the message.

Thanks to my transcriber, Kate Mears, for over twenty years of reading my scribble, providing timely proofs, and intelligently challenging me to better communicate my intent. None of this work would be possible without her patient and diligent support.

I am grateful to them all for being inspirations and companions on this journey.

· · ·

Prayer and Meditation—
My Own Practice of Intentional Consciousness

You will develop your own practice of prayer and meditation—what works best for you. I offer you my personal practice simply as an example. Over the years I've developed a practice for morning and for evening.

Morning

My morning practice consists of opening prayers, a reading, meditation, contemplation, and concluding prayers.

Opening prayers

Set Aside Prayer:

> *"God, please set aside everything that I think I know about myself, my brokenness, my spiritual path and You, for an open mind and a new experience of myself, my brokenness, my spiritual path, and especially You!"*

Step Three Prayer (Big Book, page 63):

> *"God, I offer myself to Thee, to build with me and to do with me as Thou wilt.*
>
> *Relieve me of the bondage of self, that I may better do Thy will.*
>
> *Take away my difficulties, that victory over them may bear witness to those I would help of Thy Power, Thy Love, and Thy Way of Life.*
>
> *May I do Thy will always!"*

Reading

I choose an inspirational reading from the Big Book, other recovery or inspirational literature, or scripture. I reflect briefly on it, asking myself:

- What does it say?
- What does it mean?
- How does it apply to me?
- What is the invitation?

Preparation for meditation

I ask myself, "Is my attitude one of prayerful attention?"

I remind myself of my purpose:

- To improve my *conscious contact* with God.
- To enhance my *usefulness* to others.
- To develop *humility*, making it possible to receive God's help.

I remind myself of the mystery of God.

- Who is God—"As I understand God"? Is God everything?
- All knowledge? All power? All love? All presence?
- Where is God? Do I believe God is deep down inside of me—an unsuspected inner resource?

Meditation

I use my *mind* to create my vision of God's will for me. I give it my full attention.

> *"Holy Spirit, please direct my thinking; especially divorce it from motives of selfishness, resentment, self-seeking, fear, self-pity, and dishonesty. Please clear my thinking of wrong motives. Allow me to be attentive."*

- I *think* about the twenty-four hours ahead (doing): What will I do?
- I *consider* my plans for the day (being): Who will I be?
- I *see* my vision of God's will for me today: What is my vision?
- I *decide* to relax and take it easy, to stop struggling: What action is suggested?

Contemplation

I take a few minutes to contemplate my own relationship with God. I use my will to be present to the Presence of God, creating INTENTION.

- I invite the Spirit to guide me, to have *Its* way with me.
- I respond from the heart; I consent to be placed in alignment.
- I embrace the Mystery.
- I am conscious of my intention.

Concluding prayers

"God

Show me all through the day what my next step is to be: KNOWLEDGE.

Give me whatever I need to take care of tasks and problems: POWER.

Especially free me from self-will: FREEDOM.

Show me the way of patience, tolerance, kindliness, and compassion: LOVE.

Allow today's work to provide an opportunity to be useful and helpful. What can I do today for the person who is still suffering? SERVICE."

Step Seven Prayer (Big Book, page 76):

"My Creator,

> *I am now willing that You should have all of me, good and bad.*
>
> *I pray that You now remove from me every single defect of character which stands in the way of my usefulness to You and my fellows.*
>
> *Grant me strength, as I go out from here, to do Your bidding. Amen."*

Evening

The purpose of my evening practice is to review my day and identify and remove obstacles to the Sunlight of the Spirit. I open with the Set Aside prayer.

Set Aside Prayer

> *"God, please set aside everything that I think I know about myself, my brokenness, my spiritual path, and You. Please grant me an open mind and a new experience of myself, my brokenness, my spiritual path, and especially You!"*

Meditation

1. I constructively review my day (without fear or favor).
   - Was I resentful? Selfish? Dishonest? Afraid?
   - What motives were underneath my intentions? My thoughts? My acts? My efforts?
   - Do I owe an apology?
   - Have I kept something to myself that should be discussed with another person at once?
   - Was I kind and loving toward all?
   - What could I have done better?

- Was I thinking of myself most of the time?
- Or was I thinking of what I could do for others, of what I could pack into the stream of life?

2. I ask God's forgiveness.

3. I ask: What corrective measures should be taken?

4. I thank God for blessings received.

5. I am willing to try again tomorrow.

Concluding Prayer

I close with the Prayer of St. Francis:

> *Lord, make me a channel of Your peace;*
> *That where there is hatred, I may bring love;*
> *That where there is wrong, I may bring the spirit of forgiveness;*
> *That where there is discord, I may bring harmony;*
> *That where there is error, I may bring truth;*
> *That where there is doubt, I may bring faith;*
> *That where there is despair, I may bring hope;*
> *That where there are shadows, I may bring light;*
> *That where there is sadness, I may bring joy.*
> *Lord, grant that I may seek rather to comfort than to be comforted;*
> *To understand, than to be understood;*
> *To love, than to be loved.*
> *For it is by self-forgetting that one finds;*
> *It is by forgiving that one is forgiven.*
> *It is by dying that one awakens to eternal life.*
> *Amen.*

Throughout the Day

I pray, asking for knowledge and Power. I pause frequently—and when agitated or doubtful, I ask for the right *thought or action*. I meditate. I think: What can I *do* for others? How can I *help*? I humbly say: *Your will be done!*

"Most of us think this awareness of a Power greater than ourselves is the essence of spiritual experience."

— BIG BOOK, page 568

"Simple, but not easy; a price had to be paid. It meant destruction of self-centeredness. I must turn in all things to the Father of Light who presides over us all."

— BIG BOOK, page 14

Applying Prayer and Meditation to Each of the Twelve Steps

We realize that we are inherently powerless—we have no real choice. At the same time, we know that we are 100 percent responsible for our thoughts, feelings, and especially for our behavior. Deep down inside ourselves is a faculty that *does* have the power of choice: not over the addiction, not over the spiritual malady. The heart of our choice is a Power greater than self or self-will.

We co-create our lives: our willingness, our Higher Power's Grace.

We are taken to a place of willingness; we are willing to be taken. We pray and meditate for knowledge and guidance; then we pray and meditate for the actual power to take the indicated action.

In the spirit of Set Aside, perhaps we can take a fresh look at each Step.

Step One:	We have an experience of no choice: that we need power other than human power.
Step Two:	We come to acknowledge that there is a Power, and that access to that Power is possible—through choice.
Step Three:	We can decide that a relationship of alignment with that Power is as simple as this choice and as difficult as the series of actions that follow this choice.
Step Four:	We can identify and analyze the exact nature and source in us of obstacles to this Power and realize we are powerless over these root obstacles.

Step Five:	We can fully and transparently disclose this analysis —we can be willing to reduce and eliminate these obstacles, but aware of our powerlessness to do so.
Step Six:	We can take 100 percent responsibility for the behavior that manifests from these obstacles and be willing to have these behaviors changed.
Step Seven:	We can accept that we cannot, at the root, change ourselves; but we can be willing to be changed.
Step Eight:	We can, with rigorous honesty, list all the harms we've ever caused any person or institution; we can be willing to repair that damage; we can be willing to change, to cease creating chaos; and we can acknowledge that we need power to do so.
Step Nine:	We can bring forgiveness and justice to our entire personal history, directly or indirectly, actually or spiritually, so as to create healing for everyone, including ourselves. We eventually realize the results are bigger than our contribution to them.
Step Ten:	We are committed to being vigilant and to engage in a continuous process of removing obstacles as they crop up, in order to foster our consciousness.
Step Eleven:	We are committed to a consistent daily practice of improving our conscious contact with the Source of Power; thus being empowered.
Step Twelve:	We are committed to a consistent daily practice of enlarging our spiritual lives through applying universal human and spiritual principles to guide our actions of passing on our experience to help others, especially in our respective Twelve Step Fellowships.

APPENDIX C

Twelve Step Principles—
Some Core Values

For each Step, a corresponding principle sheds light on the meaning of the Step and the actions associated with it.

Step 1: *Honesty*	***Definition:*** Honesty means facing and accepting the facts, the objective truth about reality. Honest conduct is fair and straightforward, with uprightness of character or action. Honesty implies a refusal to lie, steal, or deceive in any way.
	Action: We concede powerlessness to our innermost self—we surrender; we admit defeat.
Step 2: *Faith/Hope*	***Definition:*** Faith requires a decision to believe and have complete confidence in God, Higher Power, or Power-greater-than-self, without logical proof or material evidence. To hope is to desire with expectation of fulfillment, to long for with expectation of obtainment, to expect with desire. Hope is a desire accompanied by expectation of or belief in fulfillment.
	Action: We make a decision about *It*—our concept of Power-greater-than-self.

Step 3: *Trust*	*Definition:* Trust is a decision for a covenant, an arrangement, by which something is transferred with assurance to someone with confident expectation of the proper use for a specified purpose. When we trust, we commit to the care of someone's management; we confer a commission confidently; outward conduct is governed by implicit confidence and dependence on goodness and reliability of the recipient of this trust. *Action:* We make a decision to *turn* to be in alignment with *It*; to live as if *It* is real—which defines our relationship.
Step 4: *Courage*	*Definition:* Courage is mental or moral strength to venture, persevere, and withstand danger, fear, or difficulty. Courage implies firmness of mind and will in the face of danger or extreme difficulty, willingness to face and accept the truth. *Action:* We name and analyze the obstacles in us to our relationship with *It*—to see and accept the truth.
Step 5: *Integrity*	*Definition:* Integrity means an unimpaired condition; soundness; adherence to a code of moral, artistic, or other values. It is the quality or state of being complete or undivided. *Action:* We confess and reveal all our obstacles and secrets, to prepare for their removal.
Step 6: *Willingness*	*Definition:* If we are willing, we are inclined or favorably disposed in mind, ready, prompt to act or respond without reluctance. *Action:* We make a list of our defects of character —our shortcomings—to prepare for their removal.

Step 7: *Humility*	*Definition:* Humility is the quality or state of being truthful; unpretentious, modest, not proud or haughty; not arrogant or assertive; reflecting, expressing, or offered in the spirit of deference or submission; having a balanced, objective perspective. *Action:* We use prayer and accountability to request removal of our shortcomings.
Step 8: *Compassion*	*Definition:* Compassion is sorrow for the sufferings caused to others; it is a person's concern that freely seeks the good of another. *Action:* We identify and make a list of harms done by us to others.
Step 9: *Justice*	*Definition:* Justice is the maintenance or administration of that which conforms to law, especially spiritual; it is the honorable and fair dealing of persons with each other. *Action:* We change our behavior, repair damage, embrace forgiveness.
Step 10: *Discipline*	*Definition:* To discipline means to train or develop by instruction and exercise—especially in self-control. It is training that corrects, molds, or perfects the mental faculties or moral character; discipline is orderly or prescribed conduct or pattern of behavior. *Action:* We exercise vigilance to use this process of prayer, confession, amends, and service.

Step 11: *Awareness*	*Definition:* When we are aware, we have realization, perception, or knowledge. Awareness implies attentiveness in observing or alertness in drawing inferences from what one sees or hears; it also refers to developing a consistent consciousness practice. *Action:* We use prayer and meditation to improve our consciousness.
Step 12: *Service*	*Definition:* Service means contributing to the welfare of others, altruistic behavior. *Action:* We practice love and charity. We enlarge our consciousness and compassion, which fosters a desire to be useful.

Note: These definitions were compiled and adapted from the following dictionaries: *Webster's Dictionary and Thesaurus* (David Dale House, 2002), *The Winston Dictionary, College Edition* (John C. Winston Co., 1946), and *Webster's New International Dictionary* (G & C Merriam Co., 1909).

The Twelve Steps
of Alcoholics Anonymous

Step One

We admitted we were powerless over alcohol—that our lives had become unmanageable.

Step Two

Came to believe that a Power greater than ourselves could restore us to sanity.

Step Three

Made a decision to turn our will and our lives over to the care of God *as we understood Him.*

Step Four

Made a searching and fearless moral inventory of ourselves.

Step Five

Admitted to God, to ourselves, and to another human being the exact nature of our wrongs.

Step Six

Were entirely ready to have God remove all these defects of character.

Step Seven

Humbly asked Him to remove our shortcomings.

Step Eight

Made a list of all persons we had harmed, and became willing to make amends to them all.

Step Nine

Made direct amends to such people wherever possible, except when to do so would injure them or others.

Step Ten

Continued to take personal inventory and when we were wrong promptly admitted it.

Step Eleven

Sought through prayer and meditation to improve our conscious contact with God, *as we understood Him,* praying only for knowledge of His will for us and the power to carry that out.

Step Twelve

Having had a spiritual awakening as the result of these Steps, we tried to carry this message to alcoholics, and to practice these principles in all our affairs.

The Twelve Steps are taken from *Alcoholics Anonymous,* 4th ed. (New York: Alcoholics Anonymous World Services, 2001), 59-60).

Notes

1. Richard Rohr, *Everything Belongs: The Gift of Contemplative Prayer* (New York: Crossroad, 1999).

2. G. I. Gurdjieff, *Meetings with Remarkable Men* (New York: Penguin, 2002).

3. Ken Wilber, *A Theory of Everything: An Integral Vision for Business, Politics, Science and Spirituality* (Boston: Shambhala, 2001).

4. John Wellwood used this term in *Toward a Psychology of Awakening* (Boston: Shambhala, 2000).

5. Dan Siegel, *Mindsight: The New Science of Personal Transformation* (New York: Bantam, 2010) and Ken Wilber, *Integral Spirituality: A Startling New Role for Religion in the Modern and Postmodern World* (Boston: Shambhala, 2006).

6. Dan Sherman, *Big Book Awakening* (2006).

7. Fred Luskin, *Forgive for Good: A Proven Prescription for Health and Happiness* (New York: HarperCollins, 2003).

8. This paraphrases the observation made by Father Ed Dowling in his letter to Bill Wilson after their first meeting in 1940. Robert Fitzgerald, ed., *The Soul of Sponsorship: The Friendship of Father Ed Dowling, S.J., and Bill Wilson in Letters* (Center City, MN: Hazelden, 1995).

9. Victor Frankl, *Man's Search for Meaning* (New York: Washington Square Press/Pocket Books, 1959).

• • •

Resources

Anonymous, *Alcoholics Anonymous*, 4th edition (New York: Alcoholics Anonymous World Services, 2001)

Anonymous, *Twelve Steps and Twelve Traditions* (New York: Alcoholics Anonymous World Services, 1952)

Anonymous, *A Program for You: A Guide to the Big Book's Design for Living* (Center City, MN: Hazelden Publishing, 1991)

Hamilton B., *Twelve Step Sponsorship: How It Works* (Center City, MN: Hazelden Publishing, 1996)

Berger, Allen, *Twelve Hidden Rewards of Making Amends: Finding Forgiveness and Self-Respect by Working Steps Eight–Ten* (Center City, MN: Hazelden Publishing, 2013)

Bourgeault, Cynthia, *Centering Prayer and Inner Awakening* (New York: Cowley, 2004)

Brazier, David, *The Feeling Buddha: A Buddhist Psychology of Character, Adversity and Passion* (New York: St. Martin's Griffin, 1997)

Brother Lawrence, *The Practice of the Presence of God* (New Kensington, PA: Whitaker House, 1974)

Chuck C., *A New Pair of Glasses*, 3rd edition (Irvine, CA: New-Look, 2003)

Finley, James, *The Contemplative Heart* (Notre Dame, IN: Sorin Books, 2000)

Fitzgerald, Robert, ed., *The Soul of Sponsorship: The Friendship of Father Ed Dowling, S. J., and Bill Wilson in Letters* (Center City, MN: Hazelden Publishing, 1995)

Gunaratana, Bhante, *Mindfulness in Plain English* (Boston: Wisdom Publications, 2011)

Fred H., *Drop the Rock—The Ripple Effect: Using Step Ten to Work Steps Six and Seven Every Day* (Center City, MN: Hazelden Publishing, 2016)

Hanh, Thich Nhat, *Living Buddha, Living Christ* (New York: Riverhead, 2007)

Herman, Judith, *Trauma and Recovery: The Aftermath of Violence—From Domestic Abuse to Political Terror* (Basic Books, 1992)

Jacobs-Stewart, Thérèse, *Mindfulness and the Twelve Steps: Living Recovery in the Present Moment* (Center City, MN: Hazelden Publishing, 2010)

Gary K., *Walk the Talk with Step Twelve: Staying Sober through Service* (Center City, MN: Hazelden Publishing, 2016)

Katie, Byron, and Stephen Mitchell, *Loving What Is: Four Questions That Can Change Your Life* (New York: Three Rivers Press, 2003)

Keating, Thomas, *Open Mind, Open Heart* (New York: Continuum, 2006)

Lewis, Thomas, Fari Amini, and Richard Lannon, *A General Theory of Love* (New York: Vintage, 2001)

Luskin, Fred, *Forgive for Good: A Proven Prescription for Health and Happiness* (New York: HarperCollins, 2002)

Maslow, Abraham, *Toward a Psychology of Being* (New York: Wiley, 1999)

Matthieu, Ingrid, *Recovering Spirituality: Achieving Emotional Sobriety in Your Spiritual Practice* (Center City, MN: Hazelden Publishing, 2011)

May, Gerald, *Addiction and Grace: Love and Spirituality in the Healing of Addictions* (New York: Harper & Row, 1988)

Merton, Thomas, *New Seeds of Contemplation* (New York: New Directions, 2007)

Bill P., Todd W., and Sara S., *Drop the Rock: Removing Character Defects—Steps Six and Seven,* 2nd edition (Center City, MN: Hazelden Publishing, 2016)

Rohr, Richard, *Breathing Underwater: Spirituality and the Twelve Steps* (Cincinnati, OH: St. Anthony Messenger Press, 2011)

Rosen, Tommy, *Recovery 2.0: Move Beyond Addiction and Upgrade Your Life* (Carlsbad, CA: Hay House, 2014)

Siegel, Dan, *Mindsight: The New Science of Personal Transformation* (New York: Bantam, 2010)

Suzuki, Shunryu, *Zen Mind, Beginner's Mind* (Boston: Shambhala, 2011)

Geno W., *Sought through Prayer and Meditation: Wisdom from the Sunday 11th Step Meetings at the Wolfe Street Center in Little Rock* (Center City, MN: Hazelden Publishing, 2008)

Wilber, Ken, *Integral Meditation* (Boston: Shambhala, 2006)

· · ·

About the Author

Herb K. was given the gift of freedom from alcohol February 21, 1984. As a result of the application of the Twelve Steps as contained *precisely* in the Big Book of Alcoholics Anonymous, he experienced a profound spiritual awakening in 1988. Since then he has been very involved in carrying the message of recovery through presentations, facilitating workshops, and leading retreats.

He has authored two books to help people access the instructions and confirm the actual process contained in the Big Book for experiencing a spiritual awakening: *Twelve-Step Guide to Using the Alcoholics Anonymous Big Book* (2004) and *Twelve Steps to Spiritual Awakening: Enlightenment for Everyone* (2010).

His personal journey includes seven years in seminary, a graduate education in psychology, and a forty-plus-year career in human resources consulting, from which he retired in 2006. He has conducted workshops on a variety of topics for the Los Angeles Department of Mental Health Clergy Academy and is an adjunct professor at St. John's Seminary in Camarillo, California, teaching a full semester course on Twelve Step Spirituality. Herb completed the three-year training program in 1990 at Mount Saint Mary's College (Los Angeles) for certification as a spiritual director. He regularly provides spiritual direction based on the Twelve Steps for those seeking help with their spiritual journey.

Herb has been married fifty years, has three adult children and seven grandchildren, and lives in Rancho Palos Verdes, California. You can find out more about Herb and his ideas and teaching at his website, www.herbk.com.

. . .

About Hazelden Publishing

As part of the Hazelden Betty Ford Foundation, Hazelden Publishing offers both cutting-edge educational resources and inspirational books. Our print and digital works help guide individuals in treatment and recovery, and their loved ones. Professionals who work to prevent and treat addiction also turn to Hazelden Publishing for evidence-based curricula, digital content solutions, and videos for use in schools, treatment programs, correctional programs, and electronic health records systems. We also offer training for implementation of our curricula.

Through published and digital works, Hazelden Publishing extends the reach of healing and hope to individuals, families, and communities affected by addiction and related issues.

For more information about Hazelden publications,
please call **800-328-9000**
or visit us online at **hazelden.org/bookstore**.

• • •

OTHER TITLES THAT MAY INTEREST YOU

Mindfulness and the Twelve Steps
Living Recovery in the Present Moment
THÉRÈSE JACOBS-STEWART
Drawing on her own story and her wide-ranging knowledge of psychology, spirituality, and Twelve Step programs, Jacobs-Stewart shows us the way out of addiction's pain and confusion.
Order No. 2862; ebook EB2862

A Kinder Voice
Releasing Your Inner Critics with Mindfulness Slogans
THÉRÈSE JACOBS-STEWART
To calm a self-critical mind, Jacobs-Stewart offers an effective, time-honored approach: the ancient Buddhist practice of compassion slogans.
Order No. 9798; ebook EB9798

Drop the Rock
Removing Character Defects—Steps Six and Seven
BILL P., TODD W., and SARA S.
Learn how to drop resentment, fear, self-pity, intolerance, and anger—the "rocks" that can sink recovery, or at least block our progress. Now in an expanded second edition.
Order No. 4291; ebook EB4291

Drop the Rock—The Ripple Effect
Using Step Ten to Work Steps Six and Seven Every Day
FRED H.
Offering multiple viewpoints from people in Twelve Step recovery, Fred H. shows how prayer and meditation provide a key to a serene, sober life free of fear and resentment.
Order No. 9743; ebook EB9743

For more information about Hazelden publications,
please call 800-328-9000 or visit us online at hazelden.org/bookstore.